DANGER HAS A FACE

DANGER
HAS A FACE

The Most Dangerous Psychopath is Educated,
Wealthy and Socially Skilled.

Anne Pike

Outskirts Press, Inc.
Denver, Colorado

Outskirts Press, Inc.
http://www.outskirtspress.com

ISBN: 978-1-4327-6951-2

Outskirts Press and the "OP" logo are trademarks belonging to Outskirts Press, Inc.

PRINTED IN THE UNITED STATES OF AMERICA

"We cannot understand that which has not been given a name...."
— *Anne Pike*

CONTENTS

INTRODUCTION

❧◦❧

"IN THE END THERE WILL BE ONE EVIL ACT AFTER ANOTHER AND
WHEN ONE BEGINS AND ANOTHER ENDS WILL BE INDISCERNIBLE.
THIS IS LIFE WITH A PSYCHOPATH."

*P*sychopaths are social predators. They charm and manipulate. It is easy to be captivated by the fast-talking, seemingly intelligent and powerful presence of the psychopath. You can see that they are usually funny and fun to be with. Psychopaths of either gender are found in our families, at work, or living next door. When the psychopath creates conflict and we have a normal response of shock and attempt to remedy the injustice, the psychopath shifts into high gear, becomes alive with the challenge and all hell breaks loose on you—the innocent victim. These people wreak havoc in all areas of their lives. The consequences of their actions would fill normal people with shame, guilt, and embarrassment, but they simply do not affect the psychopath. These psychopaths continue to do untold damage to their families, friends, and business associates.

Look into a psychopath's eyes and you will see eyes that are cold and predatory. His stare is animalistic and some women believe it is seductive. Others get a chill as if they were about to be jumped by a large predator. Regardless of how you feel, these characteristics are designed to distract you from the psychopath's true intentions. Their motives are to manipulate and take without remorse. They see any social exchange as an opportunity to manipulate you, as if it is a contest or a battle of the wills in which there can only be one winner. If you are unlucky enough to have been close to one, chances are you know he lacks a conscience and has no feelings for you. His short fuse erupts into rages. Aggression is intense. When a psychopathic personality emerges, we suffer emotional and financial devastation and our emotional recovery is lengthy.

This book does not address obvious con artists or individuals with poor social skills and habits perhaps in low economic surroundings. This book seeks to educate us and reveal to us the traits of a socially adept psychopath. As we will see, the most dangerous psychopath of all is the educated, socially skilled psychopath who may also be affluent and popular. It is only when we take a long and careful look at the psychopath personality that we are able to see the classic traits. This knowledge can enable us to identify the psychopath and stay clear of these people or manage the destruction if already involved with one.

The chaos that psychopaths deliver to those around them is devastating. Their manipulations, insincerity, and pathological lying leave heartbreak and turmoil, but rarely result in jail time. Even though we know the majority of these socially skilled psychopaths are not violent criminals, we also know that they all create drama for their families and communities. By abusing those closest to them, constantly manipulating others, and blaming the consequences on others, the destruction can be devastating. A shocking reality is that hundreds of thousands of psychopaths live and work among us. Unfortunately, without being able to recognize them at a distance, they are able to move in close and prey on us.

The disordered thinking processes of the psychopathic mind are described in Stanton E Samenow's book, *Straight talk about Criminals*. For example:

> "*Certain people whom I term non-arrestable criminals behave criminally towards others, but they are sufficiently fearful (and knowledgeable of the law) so that they do not commit major crimes. We all know them: individuals who shamelessly use others to gain advantage for themselves. Having little empathy, they single-mindedly pursue their objectives and have little remorse for the injuries they inflict. If others take them to task, they become indignant and self-righteous and blame circumstances. Such people share much in common with the person who makes crime a way of life. Although they may not have broken the law, they nonetheless victimize others.*"

Regardless of what you do, what you provide, who you are and how much you give, they will eventually deceive you. The psychopath will threaten you if you stand up to his controlling and harmful behavior. We know from experience that they sense no guilt for what they do and how they hurt others and it can leave us wondering if it was our fault. We may think that we could have been more caring, sexier, smarter or less needy, because no "normal" person could be so cold and lacking in regret for the pain caused.

Some people are at risk of being targeted by the psychopath. *Danger Has A Face* gives you the insight and knowledge to be able to spot psychopaths immediately and be able to defend yourself against these predators both now and in the future.

This book identifies them as the perpetrators of harassment, manipulation, abuse, conflict and violence. The people profiled in this book are not the psychopaths who kill or rape but they have similar characteristics and leave a trail of destruction nonetheless. Based upon the experience and insight only a survivor of a psychopath can impart, *Danger Has A Face* is, above all, a practical book which could save your life.

- It reveals the traits of a psychopath so you can identify the individual before it is too late.
- It confirms and validates your experience of abuse by a psychopath when those around you do not understand.
- The volume provides answers, insight and information you need to defend yourself and enables you to find a way back to sanity, stability and safety.
- You will learn how to survive psychopathic behaviors of constant criticism, no empathy, compulsive control, charm, deviation, manipulation, mind control, mental cruelty, and emotional cruelty.
- The book will help you make sense of the nightmare of trying to live with or seeking to parent a psychopath.
- You will learn that you are not alone in your experience.
- You will be enabled to overcome the feelings of shame, embarrassment, fear and guilt that psychopaths use to control you.
- You will be provided with the means to break the psychopath's hold over you.
- You will learn how to describe to the courts, therapists, family members and others the hell you have experienced.
- The book details legal strategies you can use to defend yourself against psychopaths and the impact they have in the legal process.
- It will re-empower you so you are able to regain control of yourself, your situation, and your life.

You are dealing with someone who has no empathy, no conscience, no remorse, and no guilt. Because they have no empathy or conscience, they're natural and dangerous predators. They exhibit a completely different way of thinking, feeling and being. I would venture to say that if you did something you knew was wrong and did not feel the rush of adrenalin, the fear in the chest before you did it, or the sinking feeling and guilt after you did it, you would continue to do it. If you didn't have a conscience and if you were someone who left a path of destruction and pain without a single pang of conscience, you would know how a psychopath feels.

Some believe that psychopathic behavior occurs in 1 out of 20 men and 1 out of 100 women. A minority of experts in the field suggest the possibility that 1 out of every 10 men has psychopathic traits. Obviously there are females in this category, but we will be concentrating on males because they are more common. We must also be careful during conflict in our relationships not to quickly label one person or the other as psychopathic simply because there is severe conflict. Roots and causes of most conflict are varied and often shared.

The thinking of a psychopath, however, is very different from that of the average person. They are not like normal people. Words like 'predator' and 'evil' are often used to describe them. They know they must carefully hide their true nature because others will not accept it. They know they are different.

What I have learned is that when dealing with a psychopath— because they are different—the normal rules, the usual ways we would respond and attempt to compromise, do not apply and will not work. Together we will look more closely at the predator so we can understand how to survive.

THE STORY OF FOUR WOMEN WHO SURVIVED PSYCHOPATHS

TO THOSE OF US TRAPPED BY A PSYCHOPATH, OUR LIVES SEEM CRUEL AND EACH MOMENT MAKES NO SENSE AT ALL. PEOPLE WHO ARE ATTACHED IN SOME FORM TO A PSYCHOPATH WILL EXPERIENCE THE MOST PAINFUL SUFFERING. THEY ARE THOSE AMONG US WHO SILENTLY LIVE THEIR LIVES TRAPPED. THEY ARE THOSE WHO FEEL THE WEIGHT OF HOPELESSNESS DAY IN AND DAY OUT.

Telling the story of survivors of psychopaths is difficult. Many are reluctant to relive the horror and are worried of backlash from the psychopath if he were to find out. Those in this book only agreed to tell their stories under the shroud of anonymity. After surviving hell, they agreed that now they would like to help others. Again, since male psychopaths greatly outnumber female, I chose to interview female survivors.

Their first warning to you is: beware of people who excessively flatter you; be careful of manipulative liars. Easier said than done, as all of these psychopaths are expert manipulators. Psychopaths paint their victims as the real culprits and they have the ability to completely disregard reality.

A Survivor:

"I began to minimize my feelings and take on the responsibility for his [my husband's] behaviors, as if it was in some way my fault or something I could fix. But I came to realize that I couldn't fix his lies and his lack of remorse when caught in those lies. When confronted, he would just change the subject and talk about something else unrelated. He was always good at getting others to sympathize with what he was going through. He became the victim instead of the villain! Without bad-mouthing their father, it became difficult at best to help the children understand that this behavior was not something to emulate. In horror, I watched him take away their innocence and their self-confidence."

Here are profiles of women who wanted a way out and were lucky enough and strong enough to attempt a rescue. Their struggle for freedom was no less difficult than refugees cast adrift in tumultuous seas looking for a kinder country where they may find peace from persecution and fear. They were persecuted and are now the refugees. All of us survivors hope to provide the information and tools you will need, so together we can attempt safe passage to a safer reality.

THE STORY OF A
"I'M SCARED ALL OF THE TIME."

A is a soft-spoken woman of 34, with two young children. She was reluctant to speak and kept her answers brief. She had the habit of glancing behind herself as she spoke. This was clearly difficult for the young mother.

She began: *"While he was alive, he [my husband], was somebody who was very dangerous. I didn't even want him thinking of me. 'Don't you understand that I'm afraid of this man?' I explained over the years to*

*those from whom I begged assistance. To people unfamiliar with psycho-
paths, those words held no meaning. His recent death freed me. I could
now share my story and what I learned."*

Subject A spoke of quitting her promising career in the competi-
tive political fundraising arena to stay at home and care for her
children. When I asked if this was what she wanted, she shrugged
her shoulders and shook her head "no." Because her husband had
family money, a family legacy and a name that people in town recognized and admired, she thought this would somehow protect her.
She thought she had it all and, to her, the cost was small: a cheating husband whose anger was manageable.

*"I was in psychological denial," she said. "I had to figure a way to make
this work for the sake of the children. I became increasingly tolerant of
his abuse and psychopathic behavior. I just tried harder, didn't mention
the inconsistencies in his speech, or took the unwarranted blame without argument...I blamed myself. I thought I was the only one he had
treated like this. I tried harder. The harder I tried, the deeper into denial
I slipped. It was as if I had lost my grip on reality. I was trying so hard
to be 'perfect' that I lost myself. My reality was distorted. My self-esteem
slipped effortlessly away. Of course there was only room for one ego and
one person's needs.... mine had to go. But I stayed and tried, no matter
how much it hurt me."*

She continued in the marriage until her youngest was three. At
this time she realized his anger was escalating and his addiction
to painkiller drugs was revealing a dangerous man who victimized
her and their children. When he struck her for the first time,
she thought it would never happen again. But she admits, while
softly crying, "It never stopped." In spite of her efforts with
counseling and family intervention, the physical abuse continued
and the verbal abuse was never-ending. The situation had become

unmanageable for her and their children.

"I felt paralyzed by the challenge to survive the life that was in front of me. I just survived, overwhelmed by his sickness and abusive behavior. I became numb in order to survive. He controlled my emotions and created panic, confusion and despair for all of us in our home. I searched for ways to understand what was happening to me in this dangerous relationship. I eventually learned that, in order to survive, I could not display any emotion at all. I stopped expressing myself in my way because it led to drama. I abandoned myself, as I knew me to be. I unconsciously adapted to a destructive environment through compromise, rejection, and loss of love. I still have little left of the identity I used to enjoy."

THE STORY OF M
"What happened? What did I do wrong?"

M has just turned 45 years of age and looks older; she rarely smiles and her demeanor is sad. M was finding it increasingly difficult to focus and perform. When we spoke, she couldn't keep it together and began to weep. Her story unfolded in a torrent of misery and emotion.

She described her beginning with Rick as 'perfect.' *"He was so intense and brilliant!"* Rick was everything she could hope for; attractive, wealthy, Harvard educated, politically prominent and single. She described their first date as special, yet she remembered that Rick did eat all the food before she could have any. She really didn't think much of it because he was such a winning combination in all the other 'important' areas. Within six months, M was going through her money quickly, as she was launching her own business. He insisted that she move in with him, to aid her financial situation. In view of the fact that he lived in an eight million dollar home, it was a pleasure for M to move. Rick had told her one evening: "You need someone to take care of you." Six months later, when she was deeper in debt after paying all of his household bills, she reminded him of their conversation, expecting that he would provide financial relief. He bluntly stated, "What did you think I was offering?" This is when M knew something was terribly wrong with Mr. Perfect. M by this time was ready to break off the relationship but then she found out she was pregnant. He immediately insisted she marry him and after a quick low-key wedding at his insistence, they began their life together.

It was a tumultuous marriage from the first day. She admitted that he continued to use her to further his social standing through her parties, good looks, and warm personality, yet never once did he hold the baby. When M suggested a counselor, Rick agreed and after several sessions, the therapist told them both that Rick "was not available for a relationship." The therapist fell short of diagnosing him as a psychopath in their session. However, it was clear that, although they were married, Rick was completely unable to experience a genuine relationship. Without the proper diagnosis, M continued to feel as if the decline of the relationship and Rick's cruel and unfeeling behavior was somehow her fault.

M tried harder to please him and remained confused as to how this could have happened. None of her efforts changed the way Rick looked at her. In fact, much to her surprise, the harder she tried to please him the more he treated her with disrespect. Rick told M, "You have no friends, no family; what do you bring to the party? Look at you, you are forty-five years old and desperate!" All of her efforts at creating a home, having a child, providing parties for his work associates, caring for him, taking care of his family and being warm, honest and affectionate meant nothing. Her self-esteem plummeted.

After a year on an emotional rollercoaster, M left Rick. The emotional toll of being with a psychopath made her flee. The millionaire's parting words were "Don't forget to pay the phone bill." After two months without contact, Rick called M and asked to see her. Of course she agreed. After spending the night together, he left her and the baby again without a word and she was back to feeling her familiar self-loathing.

"I blamed myself for not being able to stop the nightmare. I sensed that something was wrong but I didn't know enough to know what it was. I began to adapt my behavior to match Rick's beliefs. In a way he punished me most when I was creative, happy and free. I stopped because it made him uncomfortable and rigid. I learned to be more silent so he would open up. I took on his thoughts and beliefs in an attempt to show him my love. My joy began to fade almost immediately after moving in with him. I began to identify with pleasing him instead of experiencing my life. I just wish the therapist had told me he was a psychopath, as I would have been able to know what to expect and know that his behavior was not my fault. Now that I have brought up divorce, he wants the baby and I'm scared of how he will treat her too!"

THE STORY OF D
"HOW CAN I FIX HIM? I'LL TRY HARDER."

D is an attractive, 29-year-old woman who was married for 6 years. She is the third wife of an older man, who has two children through his two previous wives. She is dressed in the newest fashions and she readily admits to shopping compulsively and having an eating disorder. *"It is just one of the changes"* she says, *"that happened once I became involved with Joe."* She describes herself as being swept off her feet by a more educated, worldly man who was charismatic and insistent that she marry him almost immediately after beginning to date. He was wealthy and Joe insisted she not pursue the numerous job offers she received after her graduation with honors from a prominent university. "Although I was career-minded," she states, "somehow he convinced me that he needed me to be with him while he traveled extensively."

He promised her travel, a life of luxury; he was 'too good to be true' from the very beginning. When she asked him about his previous wives and why he didn't see his grown children, he quickly told a long involved story about how horrible his ex wives were and how they turned his children against him. She immediately felt hatred toward the ex-wives and felt sorry for him. D vowed to help fix his pain and try to end the separation from his children.

She said, "I tried everything that works with 'normal' people, thinking I had a chance to help Joe. In many ways, I tried to find a balance within this relationship. I don't think he is like other people. I know this sounds crazy, but he is just different---and not in a good way.

I exhausted myself trying to fix, heal, and make sense of him and this situation I found myself in. The person who is my husband has drained me of my vitality.

It was as if Joe in some way needed the emotions of fear, jealousy, and anger to feel alive. In some sick way, it fed him. I watched him control me. It was as if he needed my ultimate destruction or submissiveness in order for this relationship to work.

Not knowing how to fix it, with no role model or how-to book available for this kind of man, I found it is impossible to do so on my own. I know from my own experience that if I could have identified him as a psychopath, I would have turned and run like hell. "

Unfortunately, most psychopaths are normal in appearance and they somehow present a picture of loyalty and goodness. But once you accept the façade and they get close to you, you begin to see dishonesty, disloyalty, infidelity and immorality. By then, it is usually too late, as you have committed to them, moved in, married, hired them, or had children with them. Then begins the process of undermining and shattering your self-confidence and self-esteem. He may convince you and, most likely, others that you are hurting him, or losing it, or going off the deep end. You are then stuck with him and forced to question your perceptions; you will ask yourself how you could have been so fooled. This process is not easy and it takes time to unravel.

THE STORY OF L

"I WILL FIGHT THE INJUSTICE, ABUSE, AND HIS LIES TO MY DYING BREATH."

L is an energetic 55-year-old woman who laughs easily and speaks with exclamation points after every sentence. She admits that life wasn't always this happy, but she believes that she has been through the worst of it since divorcing Mike 20 years ago. *"I was only married for four years,"* she says, *"but in spite of the twenty years since the divorce, it is evident that he took away my children's innocence, my youth, my trusting nature and he tested my faith."* She was comfortable sharing her story with me because she said we needed to talk about the 'dark people' in order to help other women.

"After living with one for four years and knowing one for twenty," she states, *"I can't tell you why psychopaths are who they are and how they got that way. The bigger questions are: how do I identify them and how can I protect myself? Had I asked those questions in the beginning, I would not be in the unenviable position of having my children be with him and having to repair the damage he brought into our lives.*

He made a practice of lying and cheating on me and he eventually got caught. His effectiveness in manipulating me was decreasing. Once I started to stand up and see him clearly without the veil of denial I usually wore, he wanted to move on to someone 'fresh' and newly vulnerable to his shtick. What I didn't realize was that he would punish me for the next *twenty* years for merely seeing him for what and who he was and having the courage to leave him.

After wasting years, I now know that there is no balance with a psychopath. No common ground. No compromise. My ex-husband is a psychopath who has always been disturbed, reactive, and depressed. I went in and out of a panic state, which for me was unusual. I had clearly encountered something that would not leave our children or me alone. I struggled long and hard. Believe me, I tried everything.

"Mike never gave up trying to control the children and me. Even after he married again he continued to force his power structure within our home. His distorted fears, his corrupted idea of righteousness continued to feed the hellish nightmare that he was bringing to bear on my family and me. I'm sad to say, it never let up—not once."

"I believe the three people responsible for my children's misery and my destruction were never prosecuted. It was the collision of three intense psychopaths, which led to the annihilation of a family. With purpose, he pursued me, as I had a need to help others. I *tried to* look at the bright side, believe in the inherent goodness of others, and, all the while, I minimized his faults. I took a lot of verbal and mental abuse because I held firm to the belief that I could help him or change him. All the while my children suffered from the 'conflict' that never ceased.

"I never expected to understand what had happened nor the reason why it happened to me. But it has been *twenty* years and I have learned much. On a bad day, I feel that all I am left with is emotional, physical and financial destruction. On a good day, I feel fortunate to be alive and find myself grateful to have survived at all."

CHAPTER ONE

WHAT HAPPENED?

HAVING BEEN FACE TO FACE WITH EVIL, I NOW UNDERSTAND
HOW TO FEAR EVIL. I NOW AVOID EVIL AT ALL COSTS. BUT
IN ORDER TO AVOID EVIL, ONE HAS TO KNOW HOW TO
RECOGNIZE IT.

I do not believe we learn in school how to recognize the difference between good and evil. Some people are better at this than others and I tend to think those who have firm boundaries and a healthy self-esteem stand a better chance of recognizing and avoiding evil. For those of us identifying with this, life has not been easy and I will venture to say we spend a great deal of our lives repairing the damage done by psychopaths.

Psychopaths may be unaware of the full consequences in what they do, think or act. Even in the face of requests for change, therapy or court orders, they remain the same. Psychopaths typically re-create the same situation and drama over and over again. Without true awareness and the desire to make the situation better for one's children or workplace, there is no permanent change.

The 'reality' psychopaths create influences all their relationships, interactions and choices for the future. Their world is made up of paranoia, deceit and manipulation.

The obsession with control often becomes the primary dysfunction. Their sense of self and their idea of who they are becomes the basis for their reality. Their preoccupation with control will often be the first clue, the first sign you will see in regard to what really lurks within the psychopath.

STORY OF A

"In the beginning, I would have described my husband as a fun-loving, charming man. He was attentive, sensitive, exciting, and affectionate. Unfortunately, these are the very traits that kept me from leaving him even after he started to hit me and began being cruel to the children.

"In the beginning, I actually believed Tom when he told me that he hit me because I was annoying him. Of course I stopped that behavior and the next time he yelled at me and hit me it was because I disobeyed him and deserved it. In the years to follow, I was abused because I wore the wrong clothes, didn't drink alcohol when he did, and didn't compliment him enough. One time I confronted him after he missed our son's 2nd birthday party. He immediately blamed me for our problems and after he hit me, he stormed out into the yard and hit the children.

"I can't believe I made so many excuses for him. I look back and remember that he never attended the kids T-ball games, the baby swim lessons, never showed up for school fundraisers or parent nights and when we would return home, we found him watching TV.

"As the children began to walk, they would run and hide when Tom went to pick them up. They screamed as he took them away and then he yelled at me as if I was the one to blame for the children hating him. Tom doesn't spend much time with the children but when he does, he doesn't care what is planned or what they may want to do, he overrides everyone and takes them away. I have watched for years the children's fear and my own. It knocks the wind out of you every time.

I'm not surprised now, looking back, that I married a psychopath. My father and mother were the same. But back then I didn't know what I was up against and what to look out for. I was dangerously unaware.

When you are first beginning to figure out what happened, you will see some of the following traits emerge:

- He will show off and this behavior will noticeably make him feel better. He will feel smug and more confident.
- When he loses, you will see him rage, abuse, or blame immediately, as if the act of losing somehow made him 'less than.' He needs to win at all costs.
- His anger will intensify over trivial matters. His anger, defensiveness and aggressive behavior will escalate over time.
- He will try to control everything as it pertains to you: the way you dress, your free time, your money and all your relationships.
- You will begin to see an insatiable need for power–at your expense. You must be powerless for him to feel powerful.
- You will note indifference toward the children when he is not trying to win them over.
- He is incapable of identifying with the suffering of others and the suffering he has inflicted upon others. His emotions are negative and will be in direct conflict with any attempts at creating or enjoying balance and harmony.

- His nature is obvious to others but not to himself. For a period of time, his nature will not be clear to you. This is when you must trust your closest friends and ask what they think.
- He will lie compulsively. It will start with white lies; but watch for constant lying, especially regarding what he tells you about himself and his personal history.
- Insignificant matters are blown out of proportion as he tries to pull you into his drama and get you to react. Hence, for example, pointless and long standing court battles.
- He may be conniving but will call it intelligence. Know that they are never the same.
- He will rehash the past constantly to keep the grievances alive. It is as if he needs to have enemies to feel alive.
- He feeds on violence and wants to inflict pain.

Story of L

"I knew what was happening because it became a normal occurrence in my life to have him rage and then become charming. He lied at every moment and would blame and rage if confronted. The intense stare that I once thought was passion could now be identified as a predatory, cold, unsettling stare. His secretary would call numerous times a week to ask where he was and inform me that he had a client waiting (sometimes up to an hour). I always lied for him and said he must be stuck in traffic or had another appointment that ran over, when in fact, he was upstairs asleep. When I went to wake him, he always raged and blamed me for his oversleeping, accusing me of trying to undermine his reputation at work."

Without the ability to discern and recognize lies, we will continue to struggle and deal with the psychopath's destruction. The simplest recognition of what is real and true and what is not becomes difficult to discern when you are in the midst of conflict, especially conflict with a psychopath.

In order to really understand what is happening, we must give up being passive and look honestly at what is in front of us. Look at the truth: To do otherwise leads to a path of certain destruction at the hands of the psychopath.

STORY OF M

"Why didn't I see it coming? He instantly, yes I know this sounds strange, but he instantly became a different person after our wedding day. He became so remote so quickly; I thought I had offended him to the point of his disappearance. He was completely uninvolved in the pregnancy or any of my feelings.

I was on medical leave from a corporation and trying to adjust to starting a new business at home, which was difficult. He began to verbally lash out with insane comments like 'You tricked me into having this child.' He didn't want the child and felt I was manipulating him. He called me a 'fat chick' as my body began to change in the 4th month of pregnancy. He then stopped touching me altogether and openly watched pornography for the remainder of my pregnancy.

I was a witness to a steady litany of critical comments and rage against our unborn child and me. What was amazing was that I was leaving the relationship before I knew I was pregnant. Once I found out I was with child, he persuaded me to be with him for "the sake of the baby." I made it clear I didn't want him or any financial support and I would raise the baby, but he insisted the baby and I were the reason for his being. I was to see this type of emotional seduction and manipulation many times in the years to follow.

"As the pregnancy continued, he was too busy to attend any of the prenatal classes or any of the *doctor* appointments or ultrasounds. When at *eight* months I was rushed to the hospital with severe pre-eclampsia, he visited three times in eight days prior to the birth of our child. He showed no signs of an emotional attachment as he tossed jewelry onto my hospital bed. When I asked why he chose the jewelry he did, as it was clearly not my style, he told me I should be grateful for anything he 'throws' my way and I was an ungrateful bitch. He did not care for any of my needs, as it was all about his work and his comfort. I watched him from the hospital bed with sadness as he watched TV from across the room. I waited for days for him to stop in at the hospital on his way home from work and I went to bed without a call or a visit for days.

"Our couple's psychiatrist advised me to leave the relationship. It was his opinion that Rick could not be helped because *Rick* did not believe he ha*d* any emotional or psychological problems. The therapist went on to say that Rick would manipulate the facts for his self-serving belief. It was true that Rick saw nothing wrong with who he was or what he had done. Rick felt superior and, with his money, invincible. He believed it is his "right" to manipulate, distort facts and lie to outmaneuver a perceived enemy. It is his right and he does it well because he is a self-proclaimed warrior.

"The threats that you "will never see your children again" if you file for divorce is common and begins the cycle of abuse through fear. He will want complete control over all of the family finances and all major decisions. You may be forbidden to talk with family members and friends, and the isolation makes it easier for him to manipulate you. The relentless criticism undoubtedly will take a toll on you and whoever is around you or supporting you."

STORY OF L

"I have been responding to a large and dark presence in my life that I recently came to believe is known as a psychopath. I found myself plagued by huge emotional dramas brought on by him.

At first it appeared as if the struggle was only significant in my mind-- a little thing here or there. I remember clearly one of the first incidents that began my journey back to myself. One night I made the decision that I was not going to make dinner for him, as he always demanded. He rarely made it home for dinner, but that was not the point. His control of my behavior even when he wasn't physically there was ever-present. But after days of deliberation, I didn't make dinner that night. I was surprised by the fear and dread I felt of the consequences of my decision. I kept busy with the babies but I remember being hyper vigilant to every car that passed and possible sounds downstairs of him returning. I finally put the babies to sleep and I waited. He didn't come home until midnight. He staggered into the house, loud and drunk as usual and clumsy with his briefcase. I watched in fear from the top of the stairway, certain that he would go into the kitchen and discover there was no dinner neatly laid out for him as I thoughtfully and dutifully did every night. My heart pounded and I began to shake. It seemed as if the sounds were amplified somehow in my head. I heard him belch. He did not mutter a word as he fell onto the couch. He turned on the TV and before five minutes elapsed, he was watching his nightly porn and soon after, was asleep with the TV and lights on. I felt ill. But as I stood up at the top of the stairs, I also felt different. In some ways I felt as if I had won a small victory somehow. I had saved myself the time and effort of doing a task that was demanded of me...I had won several minutes back from him. The victory was small but important, as it was the first time I had taken back something of myself and kept it for myself."

CHAPTER TWO

WHY DID IT HAPPEN?

WE DON'T KNOW WHY PSYCHOPATHS DO WHAT THEY DO.

I don't think most psychopaths know why they orchestrate such damaging scenarios over and over again to those they profess to care about. All we do know is that those with whom we choose to have a relationship have a lasting impact on our lives.

As we wonder "why" this happened to us, we must understand that, without any doubt, psychopaths are found everywhere. It is impossible to watch the news without seeing a story of a psychopath and witness his wake of destruction. Unfortunately, no one labels these people in the media and we are left shaking our heads as to why they did what they did. We search for meaning instead of recognizing the psychopathic profile and understanding that they were incapable of making any 'wise' or 'good' choice.

It is just a matter of time before many psychopaths are found out. Take for instance Bernie Madoff, who was responsible for a $50 billion Ponzi scheme. Mr. Madoff was a greedy manipulator so hungry to accumulate wealth that he did not care whom he hurt to get what he wanted. "Some of the characteristics you see in psychopaths are lying, manipulation, the ability to deceive, feelings of grandiosity and callousness toward their victims," states Gregg

O. McCrary, a former special agent with the F.B.I. who spent years constructing criminal behavioral profiles. Mr. McCrary cautions that he has never met Mr. Madoff, so he can't make a diagnosis, but he says Mr. Madoff appears to share many of the destructive traits typically seen in a psychopath. That is why, he says, so many who came into contact with Mr. Madoff have been left reeling and in confusion about his motives. "People like him become sort of like chameleons. They are very good at impression management," Mr. McCrary says. "They manage the impression you receive of them. They know what people want, and they give it to them." Most importantly, during the decades that Mr. Madoff built his business, he cast himself as a crusader, protecting the interests of smaller investors and bent on changing the way securities trading was done on Wall Street. The fallout from psychopaths will always hurt the innocents close to them. After being convicted and sent to prison, his daughter-in-law had to change her name and her children's names. A year later his eldest son committed suicide in the midst of ever-mounting legal claims resulting from his father's schemes.

By advancing their own interests, with no true regard for the devastation they will inflict on others, they jeopardize the welfare of employees and investors alike. When the truth is revealed, thousands of employees and investors will be victims through lost pensions, depleted savings, and lost jobs. Those socially skilled psychopaths who are responsible will express little or no regret. Andrew Fastow was accused of being the mastermind behind a complex web of fraudulent accounting deals at Enron and is the highest-ranking executive to be convicted in the scandal. Bernie Ebbers, formerly of WorldCom, spear-headed the largest corporate fraud in U.S. history. Ebber was convicted of orchestrating an $11 billion accounting fraud. Former publishing mogul Conrad Black and financier Michael Milken all radiated charisma and authority, but lied about themselves and their organizations. They loved the risk, did not think about the potential cost or consequences to others, and generated power through chaos and upheaval.

And here is the undeniable conclusion: they are all guilty and they are all psychopaths. Not killers. Not rapists; just cold, remorseless, manipulative psychopaths. And, this type of psychopath typically receives pardons or less harsh sentencing. They may even go on to profit financially with book deals and speaking engagements. Once again, it will be the victim who must deal with the aftermath of the psychopath's devastation.

Asking yourself why this happened to you, your loved ones or your company is part of your healing process and the beginning of understanding the psychopath. Regardless of whether it is a high profile psychopath, your children's teacher, or your husband, you must understand who they are and what to expect in order to survive.

The psychopath is usually seething with resentment, and if you fail to acknowledge his superiority to you and others, his anger will be fueled by your seeming "rejection" of him. Many women will play along and feed his constant need for validation and entitlement, but you may not and when this happens, the abuse will fall squarely into your lap.

When the psychopath chooses to be angry, it will always create a reaction in those around him. It is this "normal and appropriate" reaction from us that will trigger the psychopath and when it turns ugly, it makes us ask "Why?"

Asking why and expecting compromise or change will create conflict with the psychopath and its cost is high. Once the psychopath hears you questioning him, he will make a judgment about you and will make you feel bad about yourself. Once you question the behavior of the psychopath, he will view you as one of his enemies. Having complete control over you and having you see things his way is his goal. He will insist that he has all the answers and his pompous nature will diminish you. He will be self-serving and will sacrifice anyone who does not cater to his vision of who he is. After questioning him, there will be no win-win situations ever. Understand there will only be win-lose situations with a psychopath going forward.

STORY OF M

"He told me he was abused as a child once I confessed that I was an incest survivor. The bond was immediate and strong; it was an emotional connection. Later, I found out it was all a lie. When I confronted him he simply said, ' I thought you wanted to hear that.'

Some psychopaths will have experienced an abusive upbringing, but it is impossible to know for sure because they use emotional lies to connect with their prey.

STORY OF D

"Why is this happening to me again? He feels entitled to the best seat in first class and no mistakes can be made without an angry, blaming episode. He is screaming obscenities at the poor woman trying to do her job. I cannot feel my breath. I am not in touch with my feelings or body. He continues to yell and his kids are embarrassed. They walk away. They obviously have seen this before. I know as soon as we are by ourselves, he will blame me for the seat mix up. I am so distracted by my thoughts. I can only hear the voices in my head. My husband is yelling at the ticket agent again. I can't believe I didn't see this behavior before I married him. I want to escape."

You may find yourself making the surprising choice to stay with the psychopath out of fear of shame, embarrassment, or guilt. Many of us feel that we are responsible for the failure of the marriage or relationship. Many of us will stay in the relationships because they hope circumstances will change or, more importantly, they think they can change his behavior and then all will be well. And some, as in the story of A, are completely aware that the relationship is dangerous, but feel that they must stay to protect the children.

STORY OF A

"I know I have weak boundaries. I feel that because of this, I am vulnerable to his intimidation and threats. I believe what he says. My body is uncomfortable and it feels heavy and numb.

As the physical and verbal abuse continued, and his rage was escalating, I searched for reasons. I thought that if I knew why it was happening, I could figure a way to stop it. I prayed for guidance: 'Please tell me how I can fix this.' As the months passed, I began to feel a fear that I did not understand and would not leave me for three years. I became his prey. The children were in danger. I felt if I didn't stay, he would get the full custody he threatened and then there would be no one to protect the children."

We may believe that if we ourselves would change, his behavior would also change. We attempt to control other people and events in our environment to keep him from raging. We believe that if we can control all the factors in their lives, we can keep him from becoming angry. We make ourselves responsible for creating a safe environment for everyone. In truth, we have little control over his behavior. No matter how serious the abuse, many of us who suffer at the hands of a psychopath are convinced that we could have done something differently and that might have made the difference in his abusive behavior.

After being with a psychopath for a while, our low self-esteem causes us to doubt our abilities and downplay any successes we have had in our lives. The psychopath enjoys having us in a position in which we constantly doubt our abilities as mothers, professionals in the workplace, or as wives. Because of the psychopath's constant criticism, our judgment becomes impaired. We become victims.

THE STORY OF M

"It is not ok for him to treat me this way. Once I made that statement to myself, I tried to communicate and change his behavior by talking, making decisions with him, giving in, having help through other people, communicating through therapists and other family members, but it never made a permanent or lasting difference.

Why does he always go back to what he wants? When he does not get what he wants or your decisions for yourself differ from what he wants-he acts out. I have watched as he hurt others, embarrassed others, bad-mouthed them, made fun of them, and hurt others financially if they said or did something he did not like. I just never thought he would do this to me—until he did it to me."

Jealousy and envy motivate the psychopath to choose a popular, vulnerable individual whom he can then control. The psychopath's own inadequacy and incompetence is frequently projected onto others. Unfortunately, the psychopath's need to control you and his paranoia and jealousy, may cause you to lose or leave your job. This leaves you especially vulnerable financially and emotionally without the support of people other than the psychopath himself. When we do get enough money to leave the relationship and find a way to escape, his fear of being 'found out' and his perceived feeling of not being in control, compels the psychopath to see you as a threat.

STORY OF L

"I went in and out of a panic state, which for me was unusual. I had clearly encountered something evil. Why me? Why didn't I see this before? Did I make him this way? His rage for no apparent reason and the blaming of me was unbelievable. There was no truth in what he was saying. Could I have really been so wrong as he maintained? I struggled long and hard, until I realized that his attempts to control me and his distorted fears, his corrupted idea of righteousness continued to feed this hellish nightmare that he was bringing to bear on me and our children. It was as if in some way he needed the emotions of fear, jealousy and anger. In some sick way, it fed him. Why does he do this I kept asking myself? I know I can figure out why he is this way and I can help him change. Yet, I watched as he controlled others through his need for control. I watched as he began his most dangerous 'game'; the destruction of the children. It was his way to 'win against me. ' Why??"

Because he can.

CHAPTER THREE

TRAITS OF A PSYCHOPATH

It is imperative that we learn to recognize a psychopath before we get so close as to have incurred permanent or long lasting damage to our lives.

*U*nderstanding who they are is at the cornerstone of awareness. But, understanding yourself and why he "chose" you is also important and will be discussed. Psychopaths look for any immature, vulnerable, or emotionally needy person. These people are the easiest for the psychopath to manipulate and control. Unfortunately, these traits the psychopath looks for to abuse are also traits used to describe most trusting, loving adults and children. Anyone who has vulnerability is at risk for being exploited by a psychopath. Psychopaths will attempt to convince other emotionally needy persons to support them and they use these people as their spokespersons or 'enforcers.' Unfortunately, these people cannot see the psychopaths for who they really are and can be as dangerous as the psychopaths themselves.

You will find in the pages that follow that the dangerous psychopath will display an obsessive, compulsive, and uncontrolled aggression aimed at others-especially the vulnerable, all the while exhibiting an apparent lack of insight into his cold and calculating behavior. You will learn he is devious, clever, and ruthless in the extreme and regards most people as objects. He will display no "real" empathy although he is an expert mimic. But most important, understand he is completely without conscience, remorse and guilt. Underneath the false exterior he portrays to those of us who are trusting and vulnerable, he is malicious and evil.

Your psychopath may have some of these traits or all of them. He will exhibit most of them at some point, depending on any given situation. It is difficult to see past their act of being normal and decent. But understand that it is an act. The traits you can look for are subtle but important to recognize.

Become familiar with them and begin your own inventory. Check the clipboard next to each trait if you think it applies to your situation and let's begin.

☐ CHARMING AND MANIPULATIVE

They have good insights into the needs and weaknesses of others. They often come on strong and it may literally feel as if they have swept you off your feet. They manipulate you by pretending to understand or agree with your values, interests, goals, and habits. In the beginning they often will inspire feelings of complete trust and confidence. They put on a good show and most are willing to believe and trust in what they say and do. They use excessive charm and they always appear convincing when peers, superiors, therapists and children are present. We find ourselves not manipulated by what they say, but how they say it. You feel as if they 'know' your vulnerabilities, secrets and the emotional buttons they push will prove it. It is a performance, however, designed purposefully with the ultimate goal of gaining power and control over you and ultimately destroying you in the process.

They are cruel, manipulative people who will leave you with a broken heart and, often, a completely shattered life.

- They will manipulate you in order to obtain control, compliance, money or attention.
- They are unable to maintain your confidentiality. If that isn't enough, when they break your confidence they will typically misrepresent, distort, and lie about what you told them.
- Psychopaths are proficient at manipulating others for their self-serving interests.
- Their relationships tend to be superficial, short-lived, and lacking trust.
- Once they view you as vulnerable, they will exploit you, as "you deserve it because you are weak."
- Psychopaths are liars and vindictive in private, but innocent and charming in front of witnesses. No one wants to believe these individuals have another side to them. In reality, their true self is manipulative, lying, and very dangerous.
- They will anticipate what people want to hear and then say it with conviction as if it were their own thoughts and feelings. Psychopaths have neither original nor deep thoughts or feelings.
- After meeting with a professional who has credentials to impress them, they will "parrot back" the facts and figures that were presented to them for the sole purpose of appearing to be other than who they are.
- They are experts at brainwashing and use those abilities often—especially with children.
- These manipulators pit people against each other.
- They are super friendly to some people, rude to others, and ignore the rest.

- To those they attack, they are frequently described as "evil." The real psychopaths represent the dark, evil side but do not underestimate the power of their ability to make people believe they are the exact opposite.

If you are the target of psychopaths' attention you will you see both sides, but the courts and therapists will find him "charming" and convincing. Be aware that most people are easily and repeatedly fooled by the psychopath's charm and two-faced nature. These traits are just far enough under the surface to be invisible to most:

- They excel at deception. They are masters of the art.
- Psychopaths will always know who can help them and will manipulate these with their considerable charm. They will pursue a vindictive attack against anyone who tries to hold them accountable for their actions.
- These attacks will belittle, undermine, denigrate and discredit any who call, attempt to call, or might call psychopaths to account.
- They will manipulate other's perceptions in a charming manner, especially to those whom they need in order to protect or maintain their position.
- They successfully manipulate people's perceptions and emotions, especially guilt and anger. They rely on intellectual manipulation and charisma.
- The ability to get people to follow them is a leadership trait, but being charismatic to the point of manipulating people is a psychopathic trait.
- They seem confident and charming because of the way they brag about themselves.
- These individuals will brag or exaggerate their experiences.
- They are pushy and extremely persuasive when manipulating you.

- They have little concept of empathy and may use charm and mimicry to compensate.
- They can be brilliant, charismatic, and can radiate money and power. They can turn on extreme bursts of charm to get their way.
- It is important to not focus on the socially acceptable persona they wear, but instead see the abusive psychopath inside.
- They are very talented at appearing much more humble than the average person, but use this as a tool to be convincing.

☐ INCONSISTENCIES IN THEIR SPEECH

Psychopaths will exhibit inconsistencies in their speech and, if you are not aware, they may be too subtle to detect. Sometimes it is helpful to look away from the psychopath when he is talking so you can concentrate on what is being said instead of being manipulated by how it is being said. They are verbally skilled at twisting your words and faking expertise. Look for the following:

- They will speak convincingly on social injustice and topics that pull on your heartstrings, and then the next moment they will make racial slurs, inappropriate jokes, and/or talk about women in demeaning ways.
- They will use humor to hurt others. When the person tells them their feelings are hurt, they further demean the individual by telling them it was only a joke and that "You just don't get it" or "You don't have a sense of humor." They blame you and avoid taking responsibility for the inappropriate joke.
- Look for them to be witty, articulate, and tell amusing stories. If you check the details of their stories, you will find

they are not based in truth, but will more than likely make them look good. They will take a small item of truth and then fabricate a completely new story.

- They may ramble when trying to convince you they are familiar with psychiatry, medicine, family psychology, philosophy, literature, art, or law. Their knowledge is superficial at best and, when questioned, they will change the subject or turn their attention to questioning you—all tactics are designed to undermine others and to not be found out.

- The lies are ever-present and, along with them, are contradictory statements. They typically will go on and on when talking and do not monitor their stories for accuracy. They gauge the listeners' reactions and when someone is disbelieving, the drama is increased. They manipulate the facts to keep you in their corner. If you become turned off, they immediately will adjust their stance to be apologetic or become a victim in order to reel you in.

- They use your reactions to tell them how they are supposed to "feel".

- When speaking, they will be pompous, self-centered, self-opinionated and thoughtless, with a tendency to be pedantic.

- They often exhibit poor language skills and use negative language with few or no positive words.

- They will outmaneuver most people in verbal interactions, especially during emotional conflict.

- They convincingly intellectualize their stories and feelings. If you dig deeper and pay close attention, you will see they are trying to compensate for extreme emotional immaturity.

- If you pay close attention to what they are saying, you will be confused with their contradictory statements.

- The psychopath also appears not to be able to remember what they have said or what they committed to.
- They make big promises and rarely live up to their word. Do things they say and do not measure up? Do they speak grandiosely with nothing to show?
- After talking with you briefly, they may tell you: "You and I think a lot alike."
- They are big talkers. They will rely on repetition and regurgitation of anything they hear to convince others that they are normal. They often parrot whatever they recently heard and regurgitate the latest jargon.
- They will show no listening skills and will ignore and overrule you. You will walk away feeling as if they didn't hear a word you said.
- They are frequently sarcastic, especially in situations where sarcasm is inappropriate and unprofessional.
- They are cruel, manipulative people who will leave you with a broken heart and, often, a completely shattered life.
- They will manipulate you to obtain control, compliance, money or attention.
- They are unable to maintain your confidentiality. If that isn't enough, when they break a confidence, they will typically misrepresent, distort and lie about what you told them.
- Psychopaths are proficient at manipulating others for their self-serving interests.
- Their relationships tend to be superficial, short-lived, and lacking trust.
- Once they view you as vulnerable, they will exploit you, as "you deserve it because you are weak."
- Psychopath are liars and vindictive in private, but innocent and charming in front of witnesses. No one wants to believe these individuals have another side to them. In

reality, their true self is manipulative, dishonest, and very dangerous.

- They will anticipate what people want to hear and then say it with conviction as if it were their own thoughts and feelings. Psychopaths have neither original nor deep thoughts or feelings.
- After meeting with a professional who has credential to impress him, he will "parrot back" the facts and figures that were presented to him for the sole purpose of appearing to be someone other than who he is.
- They are experts at brainwashing and use those abilities often-especially with children.
- These manipulators sometimes pit people against each other.
- They are super friendly to some people, rude to others, and ignore the rest.
- To those he attacks, he is frequently described as "evil". Do not underestimate the power and his ability to make people believe he is the exact opposite.

INABILITY TO LOVE

Psychopaths have an inability to love, although they can be very good at feigning love and be quite capable of inspiring love from others. Once we come to the inevitable conclusion that they feigned love in order to manipulate us, many of us will require intense therapy to overcome the emotional fall out. We will believe ourselves to be flawed after a relationship with a psychopath. Understand that those who cannot relate through love can only relate through power.

- They may fake integrity, honesty and sincerity while getting you to fall in love with them.
- They have an uncanny ability to spot and use women who have a powerful need to help, mother others, or who are

vulnerable in some way. Vulnerability in others is a major attraction to psychopaths.

- They appear helpful at first, comforting, and generous; but, it will never last. They may shower you with presents and affection to reel you back in emotionally. Go SLOW if they are eager to have a romantic or financial interest in you. If it is real, it can and will be developed over time. Psychopaths use urgency as passion to snare you quickly before you have a chance to "see" them clearly.
- None of their affections are real even though they will act like they care for you.
- They want us dependent on them and will go to great lengths to make sure we are.
- They convincingly mimic human emotions when necessary to convince others of their sincerity. Left to their own devices, they will not know what emotion is appropriate, as they do not feel emotions like normal people do.
- When you witness their "odd reaction" to situations, do not dismiss this as "quirky." This is a tell tale sign of being emotionally disconnected.
- They may have numerous relationships. Often, we will be quickly discarded if they decide we have found him out and they will have a new perfect partner quickly. Some psychopaths will harass you even after they move on to another relationship.
- Eventually we end the relationship and salvage what remains of our battered self esteem.

CONVINCING AND PRACTICED LIARS

Psychopaths are almost incapable of telling the truth. Lying is like breathing to them. They will lie for no reason. Listen carefully as they skillfully twist your words and omit important facts in order to manipulate or humiliate. If you think you can catch them in a lie, think again. When you do catch them, they will simply and effortlessly make up new lies. They really don't care if they're found out, because they will change their stories so they sound even better or elicit a better response from the listener. Sometimes they lie so often they begin to believe their own lies. Some believe that simple lying can't be a sign of psychopathology, as we all lie from time to time. What we are talking about here is different. The ease with which psychopaths lie, how often they lie, and most importantly, the lack of real concern with the consequences upon others, determine if they are psychopaths. Psychopaths are very convincing and their lies are emotionally cruel.

- Psychopaths deny everything.
- You will never "catch" them in a lie as they will deny everything and change the facts. When challenged, they are adept at rewriting history to portray themselves as competent, professional, and successful, regardless of multiple witnesses and overwhelming evidence to the contrary.
- They love the drama you create by "calling them on their lies."
- Again, they will deny your accusations and will rewrite history so that they appear to be consistent with the lie.
- They will swear they're telling the truth.
- They are proud of the lies and getting away with it.
- They will say one thing one day and deny it the next.
- The results of all the lies are a series of contradictory statements and confused listeners. Psychopaths always seem to remain unaffected by the confusion they cause.
- They are evasive and have the ability to avoid accountability. They are the original "Teflon Men." Nothing sticks to psychopaths and we spend enormous amounts of energy trying to hold them accountable while they effortlessly

avoid many consequences.

- When faced with accountability or attention which might lead to anyone discovering their true nature, they will control, manipulate and punish you. Since they possess no social conscience, anyone attempting to stop them will experience an intense backlash of retaliation.
- Avoiding accountability are natural talents for psychopaths.
- They are convincing, practiced liars and when called to account, they will make up anything so that the situation at hand will go their way.
- When caught in a lie or challenged with the truth, they are rarely at a loss or embarrassed.
- Lying is a natural talent for them.
- They are very skilled at deflecting all accusations and attempts at accountability back onto their accusers.
- The biggest power trip that psychopaths have is the belief that they are winning and no one can stop them or figure out their lies.
- They attempt to distract you from the core issue at hand by false appeasement. One typical line of defense they will use is: "I know I've been a bad husband/father/CEO/employee, but that's all in the past. Seeing as we can't change the past, let's put it behind us so we can all get on with our lives."
- They deliberately lie and cheat others and although they are aware of the lies, they appear unable to distinguish between their own lies and the reality of the situation.
- They often cannot think or plan ahead for more than 24 hours. When confronted, they have a selective memory and often will not remember what they said, did, or committed to. They will tout their high morals and yet will then proceed to exploit, manipulate, and abuse you.
- Their distortions of who you are never are based in reality.

☐ PLAYS THE VICTIM. DISCREDITS AND ATTACKS YOU. BLAME.

Psychopaths hate anyone who can help other people see through their deceptions. If you reveal psychopaths for who they are, you will be the recipient of a bitter personal attack. Your credentials, lack of qualifications, etc. will be thrown at you in an attempt to intimidate you or distract you from your findings. A psychiatrist I consulted told me this about them: "Psychopaths will do anything to avoid looking inside them. A psychopath is like a large black balloon filled with nothing but air. If you attempt to reveal the psychopath, it will be akin to opening the balloon and showing the psychopath that there is nothing inside." They hate to look at themselves and will avoid anything or anyone that makes them reflective. It is everyone else's fault when something goes wrong.

- Psychopaths love to play the role of the victim. When they portray themselves as victims, we take pity on them.
- By falsely claiming to be the victim, psychopaths lure you into their deception and when you finally realize they are predators, it is too late, because they then abuse you.
- Their manipulative 'need' for you is not real nor can it ever be filled.
- They will falsely appear helpless, confused, and in need of our assistance. They have the ability to evoke pity.
- Understand the mask of helplessness is not the real person.
- Women are often drawn to psychopaths and will attempt to 'save' them.
- They may appear as victims, but in reality they are angry, lying, controlling, and dangerous.
- The psychopath receives immeasurable pleasure from provoking people into emotional responses but then is quick

to assert that you provoked him and thus they become the victim in the eyes of others.

- Psychopaths are often excellent actors and mimics.
- Psychopaths will discredit you and then will lie and position themselves to be the real victims. In reality, it is you who is the victim of their manipulations and when you finally react to the injustice of your situation, they will say, "See what I've been saying all these years? Look what I've had to suffer through."
- You are the real victim who must deal with the psychopath's manipulation.
- After months or years of abuse, you will likely be provoked into an emotional outburst, which plays into the psychopath's victim strategy.
- The genuine responses of a normal person to these manipulations and lies thus become more ammunition the psychopaths use to discredit you. You become the villain and they are now the victim.
- When you finally release the pent up anger and frustration from years of abuse, they will accuse you of being crazy.
- They fail to learn from their experiences, always blaming someone else for their problems.
- They feel no need to explain why their blame of you is justified. One of their main features is the ease with which they can blame others.
- They have history of blaming others and they can blame without remorse and with a feeling that they are entitled to do so.
- They are justified in blaming, as it is always someone else's fault. It is never their fault when something goes wrong. No incident is too small to assign blame to you or someone other than him.
- The contempt they feel for you is palpable.

☐ NO REMORSE. NO EMPATHY. NO GUILT.

Psychopaths do not experience anxiety, guilt, or feelings of remorse. Even when they have caused intense pain and suffering in other people, there is a complete absence of guilt feelings. Understand that psychopaths may feign remorse, but only because they have learned that this reaction will further confuse and manipulate others. They are completely indifferent to the suffering of others. Their lack of conscience is shocking, and it is incomprehensible that they have no sense of what effects their devastating actions have on others.

- Psychopaths do not feel remorse. Sometimes they will verbalize remorse but then contradict themselves in words or actions. They have no conscience and no regard for the rights of others. These cowards sadistically pick on the vulnerable, women, children and the elderly. Psychopaths sometimes verbalize remorse but then contradict themselves in words or actions.
- They view vulnerability and compromise as a weakness.
- Psychopaths may apologize or show remorse only to get away with something.
- They typically apologize or feign remorse only to manipulate further.
- Everyone who knows a psychopath will be stabbed in the back sooner or later.
- They are insensitive to other's pain; the weak and vulnerable are favorite targets.
- Psychopaths have no interest in your true feelings because they themselves have no feelings and no ability to feel empathy for another. They have a total indifference to understanding the feelings, needs, or pain of others.
- They have shallow emotions.

- When they are called upon to address the needs or concerns of others, they will respond with impatience and aggression.
- Psychopaths show a disturbing lack of empathy.
- They merely enjoy "pulling one over" on people.
- They are missing a sense of morality.
- Their insensitivity and indifference to others is especially evident when others are experiencing difficulty.
- They are incapable of reciprocity unless it furthers their own selfish agenda.
- The psychopath cannot experience guilt. They feel no guilt, which is why they are able to commit such manipulative, dangerous and damaging things to others.
- The callousness by which they take your life savings, or lie in court, or take whatever they want, is devastating.
- They will aggressively take whatever they want and they will do what they want regardless of the impact on others.
- They justify hurting people by assuming that others would do the same to them, if given the opportunity. They will harm others first and feel no guilt for having done so.
- Psychopathic fathers often neglect their children. They simply cannot understand or put anyone's needs in front of their own.
- They seek out insignificant sexual relationships that are impersonal.

☐ DOMINANCE. CONTROL. POWER

Psychopaths love the illusion that they are powerful. Dominance, power, and total control over others are very important to the psychopath. They frequently will humiliate friends, business associates or their own children if they start to show any independence, or they begin to become more successful or they make decisions for themselves. They ruthlessly abuse their power at work and at home.

- Dominance and humiliation are recurring themes in any relationship with a psychopath. They take pleasure in humiliation. Because they are not like other people, they are drawn to what we find obscene. They have no real connection to anybody, and are incapable of feeling true emotions.
- Psychopaths often play jokes and tricks on others to humiliate them or to assert their dominance.
- They have the desire to win and will humiliate you when you lose.
- Their tendency to humiliate and hurt people dictates their behavior and the choices they make.
- They enjoy watching another's humiliation. In a perverse way, it brings them pleasure.
- Display a compulsive need to criticize. They refuse to value, praise, and acknowledge you or your achievements.
- In order to have more power over you, they will fail to recognize your existence.
- Messing with another person's emotions and life is merely a way to pass the time;
- humiliating you is fun and enjoyable.
- They create situations to cause drama, abuse or humiliation.
- They are motivated primarily by the need to dominate and humiliate you or, very often, someone connected to you.
- They have a compulsive need to control everyone and everything you say, do, think or believe.
- Psychopaths enjoy having power over people, and they seek out positions of power because it allows them a greater opportunity to manipulate people.

- Anger is one of the ways psychopaths control us.
- As they exploit others, they must be in absolute control.
- Psychopaths are drawn to organizations or people which offer power and control over the individuals they are targeting.
- They will donate money to gain fame and have control over others.
- When in a position of power, they associate with, make alliances with, or surround themselves with clones, minions, and fellow wannabes.
- An immediate personal attack will be launched if you "step out of line."
- They will control and restrict what you are allowed to say, especially if you start talking knowledgeably about any subject.
- They will aggressively talk over you.
- They search for validation in others and will control people's perceptions of them.
- They will join boards and donate to charities and universities in an attempt to look good in the eyes of others.
- They place others in failure situations and control the situation to ensure their failure.
- They control those who can harm them or see them for who they are, and then discredit them or stab them in the back.
- Eventually they reveal their true nature, as they need to let others know how smart and shrewd they have been.
- They take pleasure in controlling the adversities of others.
- They will control and destroy anyone who can see through their mask.

🗂 SEXUALLY DEVIANT

Psychopaths are often sexually deviant. They demonstrate strange and inappropriate attitudes to all sexual behavior, attitudes, bodily functions and beliefs. If you look beyond or through the charming facade, you will see evidence of sexual dysfunction and sexual inadequacy. In the workplace, it is common for the psychopath to be extremely prejudicial and exhibit sexual discrimination and sexual harassment.

- They are incapable of sustaining intimacy.
- They carry deep prejudices against women, same sex relationships, other cultures and other religious beliefs but they go to great lengths to keep this secret.
- There can be sexual violence or sexual abuse in their relationships.
- They use the Internet as an outlet for their sexual behaviors. The Internet provides an anonymous environment for their deviant behaviors.
- The constant use of pornography is common with psychopaths.
- To psychopaths, all women are there to be used for their pleasure. And, they will tell lies about your sexuality and will deny any wrongdoing of their own.
- The psychopath will seduce you, not for the sex, but in order to manipulate or 'win' you. This behavior is a game for him.
- They prefer sadomasochistic sexuality due to its abusive nature.
- They often will demand increasingly deviant stimulation.
- They will degrade you.
- They are often sexually inadequate but will blame you for their inability to please you or their inability to become aroused.

PROJECTS A FALSE REALITY; A GRANDIOSE SELF-IMAGE.

The psychopath is constantly projecting a false image and false reality onto others. The psychopath's reality is based on distortion and lies. They see nothing wrong with their behavior and there is no real understanding or insight into their own behavior. Many psychopaths are self-proclaimed geniuses: "Legends in their own minds." They seem to suffer from a grandiose self-image. They lack clarity when it comes to their image or self-concept. They are unable or unwilling to understand how others see them and are unable to see the consequences of their behavior.

Psychopaths crave undeserved respect. They often are not professionally qualified but claim they are professional because they know of or are near a professional in the field they have targeted. They will go to great lengths to appear qualified and intelligent. Frequently they will re-write their history to appear more qualified or respectable. Appear to be intelligent but often the intelligence is focused exclusively on manipulation, evasiveness, self-centeredness and mind control.

- They often lack the ability and professionalism to be a bona fide expert. Psychopaths are sometimes successful in their field because they can skillfully fake their abilities and credentials.
- They often make false claims of qualifications, experience and titles, or are ambiguous and misleading.
- They are convinced of their superiority regardless of the facts.
- They detest anyone more competent than themselves.
- They exhibit immaturity, impulsiveness, aggression, manipulation, distrust, and dishonesty in place of true leadership.

- The psychopath is selfish and acts solely out of self-interest.
- They take credit for the work of others, and may often succeed by plagiarizing other people's work.
- Incompetence with a lack of compassion plagues them in the workplace. They may appear superficially competent and professional at their job, but behind the facade they are often incompetent.
- They want so much to be viewed as professionals but are unable or unwilling to put in the work required to achieve this.
- They have a preoccupation with their own concerns and are completely insensitive to the needs of others.
- The psychopaths friends are people who are not developed emotionally and will support the psychopath and protect them from the consequences of their own manipulative behavior.
- They may have been rejected at work for lack of competence and will feel jealousy, resentment, and contempt for the professionals with whom they used to work.
- Psychopaths have a compulsion to criticize and condemn those people who have qualifications or talents they do not have.
- They want to be known as competent professionals despite lacking in competence and professionalism.
- If you refuse to give them the attention they demand and refuse to support their grandiose self-image, you can expect immediate abuse directed at you. Psychopaths must control how others see them and treat them according to how they see themselves. They often have an overwhelming need to portray themselves as kind, caring, and compassionate people in direct contrast to their actual behavior and abusive nature.

- Psychopaths absolutely need adoration and many use pity to get the attention that they need and they will achieve at all costs.
- They will boastfully display and discuss their possessions to validate themselves and they seldom worry about anything.
- They seek envy and attention but, if denied, they will settle for your fear and hatred.
- There may be an appearance of normality but in reality, they have an inflated view of themselves.
- The self-concept of the psychopath is nothing like the reality. They are usually immature, have bad manners, and very few social skills.

☐ UNETHICAL. UNRELIABLE. IRRESPONSIBLE.

Rules and laws do not apply to the psychopath. They are unethical and believe rules were meant to be broken and rules only apply to others who have less power than they have. They will brag about breaking the rules and laugh about how they got away with it. Notice their comfort with this deviant behavior and the ease with which they discuss breaking every rule. If psychopaths find themselves without drama or conflict, they will create conflict by being unreliable. Their irresponsibility and unreliability is evident in every area of their lives.

- They have poorly-defined moral and ethical boundaries.
- They consider rules in general to be unreasonable and inconvenient.
- Will not honor legal or implied commitments to people.
- When their actions create hardship for others, it is of no consequence.
- They lack responsibility and rationalize their behavior.

- They will not take any blame or responsibly for their hurtful actions and words.
- They often deny that they did any wrongdoing or that it happened at all. If they have to admit responsibility, they will minimize or deny the consequences.
- They have an unwillingness to conform to any rules or court orders.
- They believe the law does not apply to them, but insist that everyone else play by the rules. And they will be the first to subject any "rule breaker" to intense consequences.
- This type like to break the rules. They think it is 'fun' and they are entitled to it.
- They display unreliability through erratic behavior, frequent absences, misuse of money, and cheating.
- They will not honor commitments they make to others unless it serves some other purpose for them.
- Irresponsible parental behavior is the norm. They will think nothing of leaving small children on their own, being drunk around children, and emotionally neglecting them.
- When their actions create hardship for others, they shrug off any claims of irresponsibility and attack you instead.
- They will use the law to manipulate, control, and punish you regardless of the facts or consequences. They create false evidence and state it as fact. They love abusing the legal system to their own advantage.
- Most have had legal problems for something for which they were never punished or they won in court due to unethical means.
- Psychopaths are likely to have committed fraud, embezzlement and general deception. They fool even trained professionals.
- Their destructive actions, attitudes, and disregard for oth-

ers, hurts others emotionally, physically and/or financially.

- The fear of consequences would prevent most of us from making illegal or harmful decisions, but psychopaths do not learn from their past mistakes.

⬚ ADDICTIONS

Psychopaths typically have one or more addictions. They will often smoke without apology and disregard all no-smoking rules. Just as there are no limits to their vindictiveness and the need to control, they place no limits on their obsessions and addictions.

- Their obsessive need to punish and manipulate interferes with their daily functions at work or in social situations.
- They have a preoccupation with their need to win or harm you.
- Their legal case, even if fabricated from no evidence, will consume them to the point of an emotional withdrawal if they stop.
- Many psychopaths cannot seem to stop their obsessive control of others.
- Therapists and family members can try to get them to stop the attacks, but like addicts, they cannot.
- They will continue to abuse others in spite of suffering social, emotional or physical problems related to this on-going "jihad". They will continue to abuse others despite harmful consequences.
- They will make promises they never intend to keep, and use excuses to avoid what they should do in their failure to fulfill commitments.
- They are compulsive in their need for revenge or abuse.
- Their "friends" or minions will enforce their psychopathic behavior, which leads to further abuse.

- They may obsessively collect things and may, in some cases, be shopaholics. They will buy things even when there is no need for them or the other person does not want the items.
- You may not hear from psychopaths for a period of time and then out of nowhere they reemerge to take up the cause of your destruction with the same vengeance as before.

☐ RAGE

Psychopaths frequently fly into rages while screaming obscenities. Their lack of fear keeps the rage escalating and they never consider the implications to themselves or others while in this state. If you are unfortunate enough to stand up to a psychopath, you can expect sudden threats, verbal abuse, and serious attempts at emotional damage. They see their aggressive behavior as a natural response to provocation—in other words it is never their fault.

- There is usually a history of past violence.
- They are cruel, sadistic, ruthless, premeditated, obnoxious and unconcerned.
- Some will choose to rage against you in private, so there are no witnesses and they can manipulate blame and become the victim at a later date.
- They despise anyone who can see through their deception and their image of sanity.
- They will ignore your needs and continue to victimize through raging.
- They will have an immediate and dangerous reaction to being told what to do.
- They frequently rage when they experience frustration, failure, discipline and criticism.
- Their temper is impulsive.

- They won't acknowledge they have a problem controlling their temper.
- Psychopaths rely on aggression to hide their lack of interpersonal and social skills.
- You may feel uncomfortable when they are around, as anger is almost palpable.
- Most of us feel anxiety and fear in fearful situations but psychopaths often don't feel anxiety or even sweat.
- With their temper, they can become dangerous and unpredictable very quickly.
- They will ignore probation or all court orders.
- They exhibit poor judgment.

Unfortunately, we don't know how to treat them and we do not know how to protect the population from them.

CHAPTER FOUR

THE CHANGES

THIS IS MY LIFE.

WELL, IF THIS IS MY LIFE, LET'S GET ON WITH IT AND LET THIS MOMENT BECOME MY PAST.

*I*f you live with a psychopath, you are likely to be surrounded by people who, having been chosen by the psychopath, are also controlled and manipulated by him. Not only do you suffer, but all the people exposed to a psychopath eventually start to exhibit behavior best described as dysfunctional, sullen, aggressive, defensive, hostile and/or vindictive. This not only will apply to you, but any children in the relationship. This behavior will also 'infect' new wives, friends and business associates.

If there is a person who has firm boundaries and can see through his lies and identifies the psychopath, they become the new target and he will seek to undermine, discredit and destroy them. This makes it difficult for anyone to go out on a limb to help you. They know the consequences of going against this dangerous person and will often stay far away from the conflict. There are therapists who refuse to treat psychopaths, attorneys who will not take a case if the opposing counsel is a psychopath and teachers who remain silent if they know the parent is vindictive. This causes us to have a limited support structure at a time when we need help the most. This keeps us somewhat isolated and this works to the psychopath's advantage as he can hurt you more easily when you are alone and vulnerable.

Knowing that there is a genuine lack of concern for your well-being or your needs in general will help you to avoid the shock when the inevitable occurs. Because the psychopath is untrustworthy by his nature, he is unable to trust others and, as a result, he will exhibit a compulsion for excessively monitoring you. Those who cannot relate through love can only relate through power. Be prepared for his resistance to the thought of you leaving him in any way, whether insignificant or profound.

STORY OF M

"I'm having a life malfunction."

"He was using his power to destroy me. He used his money, influence and paranoia to hurt me for the pleasure it gave him to have dominion over me.

He used gossip and spread rumors to undermine and discredit me. He was totally unable to trust anyone and this partly explains his compulsion for monitoring me. He even bugged my home...yes, with listening and video devices. I called in an agency to "sweep" my home on the advice of my attorney. They found them; listening devices were everywhere. He was relentless in his pursuit of my destruction. The shock of this intrusion into my personal life was unbelievable. He is a sick man."

"The feeling of anxiety hits me and literally jolts me awake. I open my eyes suddenly and find my heart is racing. It is almost like the adrenalin rush when one is threatened. I feel threatened. But as I look about the

room, there is no visible threat. No action I need to take to defend myself. No enemy present. Why is this happening? I resolve to stand firm and face this anxiety. I feel like throwing up."

As the psychopaths project their own shame onto others, it affects our self-esteem. One person I spoke with admitted that when she was twelve, and studying to become a nun, her father was conflicted sexually and sexually abusive and would call her a 'slut.' There was absolutely no basis in truth or reality for these projections from this psychopath, but the harm these projections inflict is very real. The exploitation is recognizable when you feel used, feel manipulated and feel very, very alone.

STORY OF L

"I feel guilt for all the times I gave him the benefit of the doubt and I believed he had changed. I hate myself for not being able to help the boys. I'm thinking back to the times I could have left the country and rescued the boys from all this craziness and the sickness of their father. I know I did everything I could. It was not enough. I couldn't keep the boys safe. They were abused at their father's house. I couldn't keep them safe. I can't even keep myself safe from his abuse."

"The boys were loving and trusting. What parent would not want to instill those traits in their children? In this case, I should have added suspicion, distance, and toughness to the list so they could have better defended themselves against their father. I know this is incorrect thinking and I should not be indulging myself in this way of thinking, but the thoughts remain. It seems the only thing that remains to see the boys is to remove them from their father and me in the process. If the boys are away from me, he will leave them alone. As long as they "choose me" (how sick is this?) he will continue to fight and hurt the boys. I am sick to think of my life since meeting him. The ugliness, lies, hurt, sickness, *cheating, pornography, abuse, anger and the destruction of all that was good, decent, loving and kind—my children and I. It seems as if I can't stop my heart from literally breaking. I cannot stop my tears as the pain runs so deep."*

Women involved with psychopaths suffer from severe stress and fear. Fear can control the mind and when you feel fear, you create perceptions based on fear. This cycle is damaging. Although most of us learn to withstand enormous amounts of fear from abuse, whether it is physical, emotional or verbal abuse, the constant drama causes us to suffer a variety of illnesses. Complaints of fatigue, backaches, headaches, and an inability to sleep are the most common early symptoms. Depending on the time exposed to a psychopath, women can also suffer from depression, anxiety, and a general sense of fear. These powerful emotions can have a strong physical and psychological effect on all who are exposed to a psychopath.

STORY OF A

"I can't sleep. I open my eyes and the anxiety I feel is overwhelming. It begins like this most days: The sick feeling that I can't pay my bills; the tightness in my chest from the fear that today will be like yesterday; the stomach ache that runs deep into my back that tells me I am afraid."

"I try to change my thoughts but the anxiety is stronger than my will this morning. I know better than to run through the list of things troubling me. I know this only makes it worse and makes me feel like there is no solution. But it is as if I am an addict with no willpower over the thoughts as they start running through my mind like credits after a movie. I can't find employment. I can't pay my mortgage. The PG&E bill is due tomorrow and I can't pay it. There is more court action. I

can't afford an attorney. I can't afford to fight in court anymore as my health is suffering from the stress. I don't have health insurance. My children are safely away from their abusive father but are not safe from their memories. I can't go on. I get out of bed…."

Some have likened an encounter with a psychopath to going nowhere fast. Some call it being stuck; unable to move forward. We all hate it when we get stuck. We know we should be doing something other than what we choose to be doing. We know we should be working toward our goals. I have heard many people say "if I were to die tomorrow, I can't believe I spent my last day on earth doing nothing important."

During times of stress and transition, being stuck is part of the process of healing. It is easy to judge us harshly. The psychopath will be happy to assist you in some self-degradation. This is not what we need however. If being stuck usually happens in times of transition, then perhaps we can say, "The more stuck we are, the greater the transition?"

Story of L

"Going through all this therapy has shown me how much I did as a mother. I see now how often I showed up in spite of my needs or worries. I see how much I gave, expecting nothing in return and how little I gave myself but how much my children received. It is an amazing journey being a parent. But, seeing the fallout from their time with their psychopathic father, I regret so much. My journey did not look anything like my dream of being a parent and having a family, but I am trying to accept what I do have and move forward with that. Not all bad, but far from what I had hoped for. Who am I kidding? Maybe not all bad for others, but it is devastating and difficult for me."

"With the divorce, our "every year" traditions were disrupted. No 4th of July tradition...no Easter traditions...no summer holiday traditions....all these events were disrupted by court, visitation changes and Dad's manipulations. The only time that persevered was Christmas. Christmas was a form of normalcy in a life with a psychopath intent on creating conflict for us all. Christmas was my chance to show the kids a normal tradition—a slice of life filled with sweetness and care. I clung to it as if it was a lifeline. I never thought there would be a day when they never came home for any part of the holidays. And now, this too is gone. I know it sounds dramatic, but this holiday kicked my butt emotionally? Loss. I hate going through it. My body aches as I suffer, but my mind knows this too shall pass."

Story of D

"My stepson stated that he felt invisible when he was around his father, my husband. My husband always told a different story and blamed his son for their emotional disconnect. During a heated argument on the phone, I overheard my husband telling his son that "Your feelings do not count. I refuse to listen to you!"

"Once I realized my husband had lied to me about his relationship with his kids, I started to ask questions directly to them and they told me about their father creating an environment where the neighbor kids hated him so much that they vandalized his property! They told me that their Father took them and their friends to Hawaii and after several days one of the friends was so upset at the insidious but constant psychological and verbal abuse that he called his mother crying from a bathroom at a restaurant asking to have her bring him home. This friend told them their father was evil. The most shocking revelation, however, was my stepson telling me that he had attempted suicide because of his father. Even more shocking was that his father did nothing once he found out. He laughed at his son and refused to let him call his mother. These *truths from my husband's children changed everything for me. I stopped listening to my husband's version of the truth and began to see clearly how I was manipulated and lied to. "*

"I am starting to realize that I have no choice but to leave the relationship that I have trusted. And I'm lost. I'm so lost."

CHAPTER FIVE

WHEN TO START TO FIGHT

"I HAVE REACHED A POINT WHERE I FEEL THAT IF I DON'T START
FIGHTING, THEN I WILL NOT SURVIVE. "

*W*e begin to struggle. We look at ourselves and see a wounded and self-sacrificing person where there used to be confidence and joy. There may be a deciding moment or a series of small insignificant things that shift your resolve to do something about the conflict. It may be his continued rejection of who you are and his criticism and humiliation of you that stops you short and causes you to consider leaving him.

When you choose to leave the psychopath, all will not be well. Knowing when to start fighting is just the beginning of a long and difficult journey. Only you will know when it is time to break away and free yourself from the daily devastation of a psychopath. Your primary concern now will be either how to manage the fallout or how to survive.

All reason and logic disappear when in a relationship with a psychopath. Abuse can be triggered over the slightest movement or comment; you wonder if you are saying the right thing or doing the right thing. The 'right thing' means whatever will keep the peace and stop the abuse.

At this stage of your relationship with a psychopath, the abuse may now reach a level where you are fast unraveling. Part of this "unraveling" may include Post Traumatic Stress Syndrome. PTSD may be a byproduct of the emotional reaction you have in your relationship with a psychopath. The relationship is typically a deeply shocking and disturbing experience. The symptoms of PTSD could include nightmares and waking early, constant fatigue, impaired memory, inability to concentrate, hyper vigilance, jumpiness and hypersensitivity, irritability, joint and muscle pains, panic attacks, low self-esteem and low self-confidence, exaggerated feelings of guilt, feelings of nervousness and anxiety. These symptoms are not likely to go away unless you disengage from the psychopath.

Know in advance that you will spend an enormous amount of time, energy and resources to disengage from a psychopath. In view of the fact that the psychopath typically spreads rumors to undermine, discredit and isolate you from your support system, it will be difficult to find some support.

STORY OF L

"It has been 20 years since I divorced him and this week he raged on me again...telling me I am a bad mother, a loser, and that my friends don't like me. He verbally abused me still on the phone and to my children. Having been emotionally abused I still find myself worrying if my children will become abusers like their father. I know they must do what they can to survive. "You are stupid" and "Look at the way you look" are typical things that are said. There are constant accusations of infidelity and consistent accusations of being a bad mother. I was screamed at, punched, and still *I thought I could* change it.

"You can feel the escalation and it is frightening. Every issue is continually talked about as he never ever lets it go. When kids are bad…. 'See, you are just like your Mother….a loser.' You become withdrawn, passive, scared, obedient, and insecure."

"I just want to do whatever will stop the abuse. You can never say the right thing…because this abuse is not about you…it is the programming of the abuser in his head. It is control…always."

"Even 20 years after the divorce…he still tries to alienate me from my children and friends."

The psychopath convinces everyone that he is the victim. Brainwashing the children is common. He typically makes fun of everything about the mother and uses humor to conceal the threat and hatred. He may never come out directly with an overtly damaging barrage, just constant demeaning comments. They will use family and friends as a neutral party to convince the children that their mother is bad.

Your life once you leave the psychopath is like having cancer: The psychopath may go into remission, but he never goes away. The threat that he will reemerge, especially if you have children with the psychopath, is constant. And if he does return, the devastation begins again. Once you leave him, remember:

1. You can't fix a psychopath; they never change, so if your life is to change, you must make it change in other areas that are within your control.
2. They appear to change with different circumstances but they are the same. We look for changes and hope for changes, but that is about us, not them.
3. The in-between-abuse cycles are when psychopaths can

be kind...such is the cycle of a psychopath and it will not last.

4. If you reciprocate with kindness, they will view this as weakness. They will then think that they are justified in their treatment of you and the abusive cycle begins again.

5. The psychopathic mindset must continue as: "Everything is good and I am still in control," or "Everything is not my way, so I must rage and abuse."

6. When the psychopath becomes upset or agitated and turns his anger on you; it actually has nothing to do with you. It is his nature to be this way.

7. No amount of understanding or compassion will change psychopaths.

STORY OF A

"I don't like to remember much of our time together, but I remember the events that led up to me deciding I had had enough. You would think the turning point would have been all his verbal abuse or the physical abuse. I am embarrassed to say it wasn't the deciding factor. When he had decided to spend a couple of weeks on a 'business trip' in London I was relieved to be left alone. However, when I hadn't heard from him for 7 days, I called his secretary who told me where he was staying. When I called it was 2am London time and his girlfriend answered the phone. Tom was in the shower and she asked if I wanted to leave a message. This one call would start the chain of events that would 'wake me up.' Of course I did not hear from Tim for another 6 days and when he did call he acted as if nothing had occurred. I asked him about the woman who answered the phone in his hotel room and he proceeded to call me a 'paranoid bitch.' He ranted about my shortcomings for exactly 22 minutes (I timed it this time) before I simply and softly announced I wanted a divorce."

"Once Tom arrived home, he was as charming as when I first met him. He bought me flowers, promised me a vacation and even played with the kids. This time, however, I felt no emotion and knew he did not want me or the children-he just wanted to 'win.' And winning to Tom meant we stayed in our place and we would allow Tim to do what he wanted to do which was to have affairs and abuse us. He continued to do what he wanted and yet he demanded that I be accountable to him for every minute of my day. He monitored my whereabouts through people, cameras, phone records, credit card receipts and counting my cash at the end of the day. I filed for divorce the following month."

"Six months later, after continued abuse, I moved the kids and the dogs to a new home that was not quite completed, as the abuse from him was intensifying and he refused to move out of our home. On move out day, Tom berated the movers and the children. On the 2nd, the day after our move, Tom left for another vacation with his girlfriend and on their return, she moved into our 'old' house and he demanded I rush our divorce so he could marry her."

Most people cannot understand why you are so upset, because to them, he is charming, if not a bit eccentric! You do not need people to doubt you at this point. If you find several people who will stick it out with you and give you critical support, consider yourself lucky.

Not knowing that he is a psychopath is the hardest part of the process. Your survival depends on knowing what and whom you are up against. Without a clear understanding of who he is, the anxiety of the situation alone will wear down your health. Understand the seduction of a psychopath is based on emotion. He will control the emotions and these emotions create panic, confusion, and resistance. You will begin to heal, but the psychopath often will not let you go emotionally or financially.

Story of D

"The old isn't working. I have become self-sacrificing. I am unable to move forward. I've lost my identity. I've lost my motivation. He continued to destroy the spiritual self-confidence I had lived my life by. His destructive ideas were punishment and the end to whatever beauty I had created. His life, the way he chose to live it, was a warning that if my beliefs became like his: holding on to false ideas and nurturing his hate, I too would suffer from imbalance, disharmony and fear."

"When I think back, I don't know why I didn't see that our outlook on life was opposite. He believed the end justified the means. He lives the reality that he must have power over life. He believes he must have an advantage over others and he frequently uses sarcasm and put-downs. He attacks and believes he is clever because of the hurt he can inflict with his superior intellect.

Force over wisdom is his decree. He believes in taking what is rightfully his-even if it means people or feelings. He doesn't feel and he doesn't care how people feel or how his actions affect others. He must win at all costs. Seeing as I was involved with him, I went down with the ship-so to speak. When I asked what is this person really like apart from his ability to charm and be successful-what is in his core? I have to admit that I was disappointed I had chosen *so* unwisely. "

Years later you may still think that you can handle a psychopath or you can make him understand but it will never happen and that is the sorry truth. Psychopaths are preprogrammed and you can never change the programming.

STORY OF M

"Once I realized that taking my own life was not the answer and I knew I was meant to see this through, something changed. I searched for words that fit the experience and they eluded me. "

"As this state of mind stayed with me, I recalled a scene I witnessed when I was 10 years old and living at the beach, and it became the information that would save my life. When we lived there, we had a friend who was an extreme risk taker and he was frequently found praising himself for his skill at defying the odds of being a victim of rip tides, sharks or poisonous jellyfish. He apparently was a very strong swimmer and prided himself on being tough. As the story goes, on this particular day, he was swimming and he encountered a rip tide, which is a very strong undercurrent in the ocean. Fear must have taken over, because by all accounts from witnesses on the beach, he struggled. He struggled fiercely. When this was told to the group, most of the adults shook their heads in agreement and uttered; 'Yes, what else would one do in this case? Good thinking to fight! Brave man.' A few of the adults dropped their heads, as if they knew what was coming next in the story. The sad story continued; the man was no match for the rip tide, regardless of his efforts to fight it and it held him under the water and carried him out to sea. No one saw him again."

"The few adults that seemed to know why this had happened whispered in the corner of the room. I gravitated to them, as they were different than the others. I came within earshot, as it is so easy to do as a child, and heard them say, 'It's just like him to think he could beat it.' 'If only he had stopped struggling, he would have popped up like a cork.' Could this be true? I had no reason to doubt the few who stood silent and did not participate in the drama un-folding in the house. This was my first lesson in surrender."

"I thought of this often when I was trying to make sense of the bigger issue underlying the principle of surrender. When I sur-rendered to my experience of betrayal, abuse and deception, I began to find acceptance in that which was unfathomable and would had consumed my mind and my days. I began to feel more strength. When I struggled less, I seemed to 'pop up,' as if out of a rip tide of depression and oppression. To hear others remark upon this time, they would frequently use the word 'courage' to describe what they witnessed in me. I thought of it as survival."

"I had awakened from a very bad dream. I had gone deep into my own personal hell and I suffered in order to acquire awareness. Hell was a mental state for me, and created by me. I had 'decided' to wake up. Could my reasoning keep my options limited? I felt a creeping clarity in the midst of this suffering. I felt I had the power to change everything even in the face of insurmountable odds, but would it work? Could I make it? I prayed I would trans-form this ugliness, my life, into a happy story that I could pass on to my children. My life to that point was characterized by fear and it no longer held me tight. Could surrender be that important? I know the 'rip tide' of my personal hell held me down until I was able to surrender and only then did I 'pop up out of the rip tide' and breathe again."

The psychopaths will exhibit behaviors that are typically not il-legal, but behaviors that are damaging and unethical. When psychopaths cheat on a wife, or hurt them financially, and emo-tionally abuse them, it is difficult to prove and often they have little or no legal recourse. It is typical of psychopaths to skate around the law through manipulation of the court and city officials. These abuses however, are not considered a crime.

STORY OF A

"I did not know the true profile of a psychopath or that my husband was one of them at the time of my divorce. I knew things were very wrong. I knew he was sick and dangerous and it would not get better. I did not know enough about the profile of the psychopath to know that I should have been very afraid of his threats of revenge."

CHAPTER SIX

WHAT YOU CAN DO

"ALL THAT IS ESSENTIAL FOR THE TRIUMPH OF EVIL IS THAT
GOOD MEN DO NOTHING."

-EDMUNDE BURKE

*F*or those of us who have decided to move away from the control of the psychopath, the plan is now damage control. We can attempt to minimize the harm we experience going forward—hope for a temporary fix of the damage already done. And we will experience harm in one or several ways: abuse, degradation, violence, humiliation, financial abuse, lies and blaming. There are steps and defense strategies to take before you leave a psychopath, which may help you once you have left.

Wanting to leave and then making the decision to leave does not mark the end of your relationship with the psychopath. Even after all your efforts, he may never go away and if he does, he may pop up on the radar from time to time to create more drama and abuse. There may be years of frustration and demands on your life due to the psychopath's interference. Psychopaths are angry at not getting what they want and furious over the lack of control. This will not be a one-time threat. This situation can be ongoing or intermittent for upwards of 20 years or more. Know this so you can be prepared and armed with realistic expectations. You must develop a strategy to prepare yourself for the anger, retaliation, and abuse that will most likely come your way.

If you are in this situation, and you have attracted a psychopath, you are susceptible to being vulnerable. Do not let his manipulations make you doubt yourself, or lure you into making compromises, as these compromises you make now may harm you in the future. Often we make decisions that are fair, but we forget that the psychopath will view compromise as weakness and your good intentions will fuel his attacks on you.

In order to rescue yourself, what you can and must do is learn to recognize the psychopath and know that the psychopath routinely manipulates even experts. Learn who he is and you can then protect yourself. We must know what a psychopath is, , how to identify them, and how much damage they can do. We know that the majority of psychopaths milling around who are not in jail are the most dangerous. The only protection you have is self-protection through self-education.

Remember that your pain has been from the psychopath's abuse, manipulation, lies and constant criticism, and your suffering is real. His 'suffering' is a ploy to manipulate you and get what he wants. It bears repeating that they are incapable of empathy and compassion unless it is acting 'as if' they possessed the skill. They use this acting 'as if' ploy with therapists, courts, friends and co-workers. Do not underestimate the inability of others to see them for who they truly are. Do not have sympathy for them. They are not suffering. They are incapable of feeling what you are feeling. Know this simple truth as you move on.

It is also time to stop suffering in silence. It is time for you to talk about it. You must not keep this information inside. I know you are feeling stupid, foolish or embarrassed to have put yourself in this position. Get over it and share. Get support. And, believe me, you are not alone. You may feel like withdrawing, but know that no one can escape the journey. There may be an exodus of 'friends' from your life as this promises to be a long and ugly journey. But just as you lose some friends, you will gain others. As you change, so will your relationships and eventually you will have true and strong friends once you become free of the abuse from the psychopath.

When being barraged with the intense verbal style of the psychopath, shut your eyes or turn your head. Listen carefully to his words without being mesmerized or distracted by his seductive performance. Listen carefully to what is being said and look for inconsistencies and lies. The signs will be clear so trust your instincts. Ask questions. Ask more questions than you normally would. If the answers are vague or inconsistent, be suspicious. Being a detective in this effort at the beginning could save you from additional humiliation and abuse.

Know yourself. Look inside yourself. Taking responsibility for the part you played without self abuse and regret is most likely more difficult than standing up to a psychopath. Why? Because this is a new pattern, a new way of being and it must be learned in order to go on. If I said that unless you learned a new way to think and be, you could attract another psychopath into your life, would you then give this a try? My guess is that you not only would give it a try, but you would make it a priority in your life!

A fearless moral inventory is difficult under the best circumstances, but is critical in identifying and protecting yourself from a psychopath. Know your own weaknesses, because the psychopath will find and use them. Are you lonely? Are you in a vulnerable transition? Do you have a co-dependent nature? Do you need to mother others or need flattery? Understand yourself, your limitations and your weaknesses; he will prey on them and exploit you by using them. No boundaries are acceptable to those of us who have been trained to accept intrusions. We accept being violated in some way, as this has frequently been the pattern in our lives. Be especially cautious during difficult personal times, especially when meeting someone new. If the person notices and comments on your state of mind, your sadness, your homesick feelings, your loneliness, know that he is aware of your vulnerabilities for a reason. A normal person will be truly sympathizing, but a psychopath will be scheming to manipulate those weaknesses. You need to look for and expect insights from these difficult times. You now know that you must be friends with your own weaknesses because the psychopath will find and use them.

Let us hope you have committed to stop suffering in silence and move away from the control of the psychopath. I trust you have realized that in order to rescue yourself you need to know what a psychopath is, how much damage psychopaths do, and how to identify them. This is a very good start. And even if you did nothing else, this would help you to not attract a psychopath again in your life. At this point, you know enough to protect yourself from another encounter. We need now, however, to discuss what to do next to manage the damage with the psychopath who's still in your life.

To minimize the harm from the psychopath in your life, know what to expect:

✚ **Self Defense Strategy**: Pay attention to everything! They hide the dark side of themselves and the faster you uncover it, the sooner you can spare yourself the pain that comes with this type of person. Quietly verify what he says. The grain of truth he drops occasionally is deceptive manipulation. Do not try to negotiate or bargain. Head for the door when things don't add up.

✚ **Self Defense Strategy**: Recognize his patterns so you avoid being 'in shock' when the inevitable abuse occurs. Seeing it coming allows you to remain clear headed and non-emotional. Allow yourself to feel, think and act. Use your good judgment.

✚ **Self Defense Strategy**: Don't tip your hand that you're leaving. When telling a psychopath that you are leaving, the chance of violence rises. Protect yourself with a restraining order if needed. Do not allow him to talk you out of protecting yourself with whatever means you need to BE SAFE.

✚ **Self Defense Strategy**: Say NO to abuse! Act to protect yourself physically, financially, and emotionally. Pay attention to when and where you are uncomfortable with him. Have a clear understanding regarding what amounts to unacceptable behavior with clear consequences. Know your fight or flight options.

✚ **Self Defense Strategy**: Be prepared. Be aware of the services of the police, the law and shelters. Commit and follow through. Stay in the present. If married to him, prepare for a nasty divorce.

✚ **Self Defense Strategy**: Avoid him when your gut instinct tells you to avoid him. Know that his goal is your attention, and controlling or abusing you. Expect him to try to degrade you. Honor your discomfort. Trust your feelings. Pain drives us to change. Your gut instinct will tell when you are in danger and you should pay attention and GET OUT.

✚ **Self Defense Strategy**: Abandon your efforts to help or cure him. Accept the reality. Know his ability to appear helpless, pitiful, confused and needing our assistance.

✚ **Self Defense Strategy**: Ignore and don't react to his hurtful words. Don't take the bait when he blames or lies. Don't take the bait of his rage or manipulation. Get away from him.

✚ **Self Defense Strategy**: Do not be vulnerable or naive. We know that it is common for psychopaths to overwhelm you with flattery, kindness, affection and gifts immediately after telling him you are leaving. Do not slip into denial. No making 'nice, nice.' Don't change yourself to match other people's feelings and situation. If he won't give reasonable answers to reasonable questions turn and run. Run!

✚ **Self Defense Strategy**: Contrary to what the abuser will tell you, you do have power and you do have control over your life. Take positive action every day to move your life forward--without fear. Use the power of momentum and develop habits that take you in the direction you want.

✚ **Self Defense Strategy**: Get professional advice and help for yourself only. Do not attempt to save the psychopath. Saving yourself will be a full time job. No need to defend or rescue anyone but yourself. Join a support group to know you are not alone

✚ **Self Defense Strategy**: Get everything in writing. You will enter into a power struggle with every item that is not

clearly agreed to in writing. Expect him to fight you on
every issue. Ask for more than you want because you will
have to settle with a psychopath. Expect him to disregard
any and all agreements. Remember: he has to win.

✛ **Self Defense Strategy:** Strive to keep stability in your
home, especially if children are involved. Continue to
maintain integrity and high moral standards for yourself
and with your children.

✛ **Self Defense Strategy:** Call the police and document all
abuse. Document thoroughly to protect yourself. Let the
professionals help you with a plan. If you don't have evidence, the psychopath will convince the attorneys and
therapists that it is you. You must have proof and evidence
of his psychological, verbal, physical, and financial abuse.

✛ **Self Defense Strategy:** REMEMBER: WITH THEIR
DYING BREATH, PSYCHOPATHS WILL DENY
THE TRUTH EVEN WHEN PRESENTED WITH
IRREFUTABLE EVIDENCE TO THE CONTRARY.

STORY OF D

"He admitted to cheating on his first wife constantly over the 15
years they were married. She even got pregnant after 5 years of
marriage and he convinced her to have an abortion even though
she wanted the baby. You would think I would see the facts and run
like hell away from him, but the way he told it made me feel like
she was a terrible wife and he was justified in cheating. He created
an environment where the levels of denial were so great that I was
oblivious to the lies and absurdity of his stories. When I eventually
found out the truth, and I presented him with the facts, he contin-

ued to deny the truth! After a while I thought I had gone crazy and I thought I needed psychiatric intervention."

In spite of the devastation to you and your family, the actions of a socially skilled psychopath may go unnoticed by others. Do not expect others to see what you have been through. In fact, often psychopaths will use their money in the community and in positions of influence, and those organizations or individuals choose not to see who he really is, as their primary concern is the money. They may turn a blind eye to his abuses of you and/or your children and believe it is not relevant in their business transactions with the psychopath. It may take years, if at all, before others finally expose the psychopath and the full extent of the destructive behavior can be seen.

CHAPTER SEVEN

OUR LEGAL SYSTEM AND THE PSYCHOPATH

~⁓⁓

THE PSYCHOPATHS' APPROACH TO LIFE IS SO DRASTICALLY DIF-
FERENT FROM OURS THAT WE ARE COMPLETELY UNPREPARED TO
DEAL WITH THEIR SICKNESS IN OUR LIVES.

*E*ntering into the legal system with a psychopath is a slip-
pery slope and one that requires all your mental efforts.
Unfortunately, if the psychopath has done his job well, by this
time, you may feel beaten down. In order to make the correct decisions for yourself, you must find the strength to understand what
to expect. We have learned from earlier chapters, but it begs to
be restated: When our world includes dealing with psychopathic
individuals, these people feel a need to win at all costs. Read this
again. Psychopaths need to win at all costs. Although he may state
with conviction that it is about the truth, this is not the case, neither is it about what is best for the children or about fairness and
compromise. If you assume that the psychopath and the courts will
try to do the right thing and be fair and honest, that belief will be
your downfall. This is about winning. They equate winning with
power. They must control and be in charge. They have to control
you, the children, the courts, the therapists and the mediators.

As the conflict escalates between you and the psychopath, you may find it difficult to find any person or professional who knows how to protect you from this individual. It is likely that your attorney will not recognize a psychopath and will encourage you to fight because you probably have a great case against him. Only you will know he is a psychopath and, in fact, dangerous. Do not expect to have your attorney, sister, or friend understand this. Because our friends and family may not have experience with psychopaths, the advice they give may not be effective and can actually hurt you.

You are risking serious emotional and financial consequences and trauma by going to court against a psychopath. You may be under the misguided belief that the courts will 'see the light' and treat you fairly and, in most cases, this may be true but not with a psychopath. You can expect the family court system to not acknowledge his psychopathic traits because of his 'charming' personality and his treacherous ability to make you the abuser and himself the victim in the eyes of the court. It may be best to cut your losses, but if you give in too easily, he will take advantage of you even more.

The psychopath will receive pleasure from provoking you into engaging in conflict. And, once conflict has been initiated, the psychopath gains increased gratification by exploiting your instinctive need to retaliate or protect. If you have children, it is even easier for the psychopath to do something horrible to you or your children and sit back and wait for your outrage. Once you act appropriately with anger and boundaries, he uses this to twist the truth and make you look unstable, hostile, or to bring up a host of other psychological issues. The game he plays assures escalating conflict, and the destruction of you, your children, and your family.

STORY OF L

"A year after my divorce was final, the ex had remarried the woman he met in a bar in London and, within months, she had called the police after he physically abused her. After his arrest, he had a trial pending. He was not seeing the children, as he refused to exercise his visitation *privileges*. After 2 months of not seeing our children, I asked him what was happening and he told me he was having a breakdown. The children did not want to see his new wife and they had very negative reactions when her name was mentioned. We agreed to go to mediation to discuss the issues facing the children. Mike proceeded to cry in the mediation and blame me for not letting him see the children although he had not made any attempts to participate in his visitation. The mediator listened as Mike cried, "I know I have been a bad father but I will do better...just give me a chance...I can't lose my children!"

"The mediator seemed to melt and suggested that I give him a second chance. This worked so well for him that he used the same ploy numerous times with therapists, judges, mediators and evaluators. Every time, they had the same reaction as the initial mediator and they recommended that I give him a second chance. Oh yes, the repentant father angle. If I didn't give him another chance, I looked harsh, unforgiving and unreasonable. This was his "get out of jail free" card and he continued to abuse, neglect and hurt the children and me for 18 more years. When I called him on his abuse or neglect of the children, he used the same tactic and was released from consequences. The only people who suffered were the children and *me*, as we were never given a break from his abuse. We were consistently told to be understanding and forgive his behavior. His abusive behavior was renamed as 'slights,' 'temporary lapses of judgment,' 'understandable reactions to stress' and 'normal behavior under the circumstances,' and yes, he was just given another 'pass.'

While we endured his *I-am-the*-victim rhetoric with the therapists, the children and I continued to suffer indefinitely."

You cannot change the psychopathic personality, but there should be attempts-in the beginning to modify their behavior by convincing them that there are ways they can get what they want without harming others. Because we are reasonable and compassionate people, we must try everything before we resort to giving up on a loved one completely. You can try to make the psychopath understand that violence is bad, not *just* for you or the children, but also for the psychopath himself. If it works, well done. If it does not, read on.

STORY OF A

"When I think about my experiences with the psychopath, I recall never having enough: not enough peace, love or joy. And not enough of the little things like kindness, someone to listen, and someone to touch me with genuine affection. When it was dinnertime, we all ate fast because there was so little happiness at the table. There was tension and emotional outbursts from him constantly. I remember being hungry all the time. I think of the lies. I remember being told "Everything is OK,," *when* I clearly knew it was not. But when I asked again, the answer was always the same, "Don't be so sensitive, what's wrong with you?" But I continued to try in hopes that our family could be fixed or salvaged."

If you choose to take charge of your life, you must be prepared for a dangerous and damaging fight. In fighting back, you may learn how to empower yourself or face the demons that helped create this situation in the first place or it could be the demise of all you worked so hard to build in your life. You may risk losing everything.

THE STORY OF L

"The fear seemed to become bigger and more intense when I shared it. When the attorneys were involved, the fears had a life of their own. I needed to strategize in order to fight the fear. I had to posture in order to calm the fear. The more the fear was projected onto my children and me the more it continued to grow. It was as if the fear was a cancer and we fed it cancer food, every day."

MYTHS WHEN DEALING WITH A PSYCHOPATH:

1. Things will get better
2. The court, therapist, and/or mediator wants what is in the best interests of the child
3. The court, therapist, and/or mediator will see through the psychopath's lies and manipulations
4. Time heals all wounds
5. You can control your reactions, thereby you have control
6. The psychopath will do the right thing by the children
7. The legal system is fair
8. Being right is important
9. What is right is worth fighting for
10. The truth shall set you free
11. You can rise above it
12. It will eventually end
13. This too shall pass
14. If people do the right thing, there's no basis for any lawsuit
15. It's about doing the right thing
16. You will win with:
    • Good representation

- The truth on your side
- Enough facts
- Enough money
- The children wanting to be with you
- Love on your side
- God on your side

STORY OF **L**

"The judge in family court listened for over a year to all the evidence and finally when it came time to settle she had the ex go outside and she told me and my attorney, 'I know you are an A parent and he is a F parent, but overall, the kids will have a C experience.' This was an acceptable outcome to the court. In reality, she didn't believe I was as good a parent as was being said and he wasn't as bad a parent as was being proven. Court was all about compromise. Had I known this before, I would never have put the future of my children in the hands of family court."

WHAT YOU CAN EXPECT-COURT STRATEGIES:

Court Strategy: Be prepared before going to court. Do not assume because you are right and he is wrong that you will not need to bring evidence to support this. A psychopath is almost always wrong, but don't expect the therapist or courts to understand this. The courts still believe that the truth always lies somewhere between the two extremes; one person cannot be 100% bad and you most likely will not be believed to be all good. Courts believe guilt is shared 50/50.

Court Strategy: Do not listen to anyone saying, "If people do the right thing, there's no basis for any lawsuit." They obviously do not have experience with psychopaths. If it takes $100 to tell the court a lie, it will cost $300 to prove that the allegation is a lie. Be prepared to pay dearly to prove your innocence and prove that you are a good mother.

🏛 **Court Strategy:** Do not waste your time and money with an attorney who specializes in mediation or who is not adept in the courtroom. Expect the psychopath to ask for confidential mediation, and expect them to abuse you in the session because the mediator cannot report his behavior to the court. The psychopath will fight for mediation so as to give the impression in public that they are negotiating and he is the perfect husband or father. The reality is that they will continue with the harassment and abuse in private. Find attorneys, therapists and judges who have experience and can understand the games a psychopath and his attorney will play.

STORY OF A

"The very first thing the court said was that we attend mediation. Of course I complied and when I arrived at the mediators, he glared at me in the waiting room. He began his verbal attacks on me as soon as we were in her office. Finally, when I realized she wasn't going to stop it, I stood up and walked out of her office. He followed me all the way to my car ranting and raving and blaming me for his troubles. I had hoped the mediator would tell the court what she saw, but I learned *it was confidential mediation* insisted upon by the ex and his attorney. I didn't attend the remainder of the sessions and it was presented in court that because of this, I was unwilling to try to make things better for my children. The judge verbally reprimanded me for my lack of compliance."

🏛 **Court Strategy:** Mediation with therapists or in court will be a waste of time with the psychopath. They will use any negotiation to exploit you further. Many therapists have remarked that they refuse to treat psychopaths and in their opinion, they cannot be cured. They will use therapy to gain new excuses and rationalizations for their behavior. They may use therapy to learn new ways of manipulating as you are vulnerable in session and he will take full advantage of the disclosures to abuse you further.

🏛 **Court Strategy:** This legal attack is viewed as war to the psychopath. If your psychopath has money, a personality disorder, a current wife or friends who are hateful, your success using compromise and mediation is severely unlikely. A psychopath with money and "a hateful group of advisors" is like pouring gasoline on a raging fire.

STORY OF L

"My ex remarried immediately after our divorce to a much younger woman. She was poor and from "the wrong side of the tracks" so to speak and she would do anything for the money and prestige my ex had to offer her. It was only natural that she became his enforcer. She would take the children aside and tell them how sorry she was they had a mother like me. She filled them with lies about me and told the therapists she witnessed abuse from me towards the ex, none of which was true. She 'recruited' a few friends and, together, they became my worst nightmare. The ex used her to carry out his manifesto of abuse and he looked like the good guy to the children."

🏛 **Court Strategy:** Protect yourself and your children before you or your attorney threaten "enough is enough" to a psychopath. This will be misread by psychopaths and will escalate the conflict. His retaliation will be quick and lethal. His intent to harm overrides any caution and reason—even against his own attorney's advice. He will not follow any court or therapist's recommendations and there will be no consideration of the consequences and the lasting harm to you or your children. Before you escalate with a psychopath, be prepared and protected.

🏛 Court Strategy: No one can negotiate or bargain with psychopaths. Do not waste your time, money, or efforts on compromise or compassion. To normal people, compromise and compassion is a positive trait. To a psychopath, those attributes are a sign of weakness.

🏛 Court Strategy: Do not give in to panic, anger, or retaliation. Remember this and believe me when I say that the psychopath finds joy and gets immense gratification from causing you distress.

🏛 Court Strategy: Every criticism and untrue accusation they will make about you is really an admission about themselves. Know this. Instead of being shocked and hurt at the lies, begin to accumulate evidence of his behavior in the same areas he is accusing you. When the psychopath makes a contention of abuse or neglect, you can be certain that he has committed some form of abuse in his past. Most psychopaths have a past, which includes some criminal activity; spousal abuse, fraud, compulsive lying or anger issues. Do your detective work. Be thorough. Make these facts part of your legal strategy. Knowing the psychopath's past and getting it admitted into court will be a fight. Once admitted, expect the psychopath to become the victim.

STORY OF M

"I was shocked when I heard him say he was sorry for his abuse and even more shocked as I watched how the court felt sorry for him. He played the repentant Dad role perfectly and they loved it. Once he saw it was working he continued with 'I'm sorry; it was a long time ago and I wasn't perfect. I learned *from* my mistakes and I will never do it again.' What was completely unreal was how he turned it on me by saying 'I keep saying I'm sorry and I've shown her I've changed, but she just won't give me a chance with our children. The court ruled in his favor after that and my child has been suffering ever since due to his continued abuse."

🏛 **Court Strategy:** When psychopaths are revealed, they may claim that you are 'mentally ill' or 'mentally unstable.' As part of your defense, be prepared to tell the court first that it is the psychopath who is unstable or ill. Do not take the "high ground" and leave this information for the psychopath to use.

STORY OF A

"I felt that if I told the whole story in court, my children would find out someday about their father and I didn't want them to know who he really was. In trying to protect my children and their relationship with their dad, I lost my opportunity to protect them by getting custody in court. My consideration of their feelings was my undoing in court-he won by telling the court that I was abusive, neglectful and unstable. In reality he was all of those things but because I never stated it-he used it against me. I lost everything."

STORY OF M

"My attorney told me to dig into his past. I thought it was a waste of time because he said he had told me everything about himself. I was horrified when the agency showed me proof that he had been arrested before for spousal abuse and that he had an arrest record for intimidating a witness and providing false testimony. He also had several DUI's and had been ordered to attend anger management classes. I couldn't believe it. Everything I thought I knew about him changed in an instant."

Court Strategy: Psychopaths are skilled at using the courts for their own devious purposes and are so convincing, they are typically the ones who are believed. Remember: psychopaths lie like they breathe. They will manipulate the truth and find it exhilarating to make you look bad. The psychopath's truth will be corrupted in order to manipulate and win at all costs.

STORY OF L

"When I read his first court declaration I laughed and told my attorney that they were all lies. Every statement was a lie. Completely made up. Both my attorney and I after that moment felt confident that without proof and such obvious lies, we would win easily. What a mistake that strategy turned out to be! The judge believed him-even without a shred of proof. I lost custody based on his lies. He destroyed a good family just for the fun of fit. My kids were devastated. He doesn't spend any time with them. He just wanted to win."

Court Strategy: Because of the psychopaths' personality disorder, they are compulsive liars and you need to push for the fact that their testimony cannot be believed under oath and in court. Fight for this.

Court Strategy: With a psychopath as an adversary, avoid depositions. These are stressful enough for the normal person and because we are under oath, we feel we must reveal everything. However, as we've shown, psychopaths are liars and swearing under an oath means nothing to them. They will avoid answering the questions or give long winded explanations that have nothing to do with the question.

Court Strategy: In normal circumstances, you can honestly admit your mistakes, but with psychopaths, they will completely distort whatever you admit to and they will claim no wrongdoing about anything, ever. The normal rules of fairness and honesty do not apply with a psychopath. The truth will always be distorted and his intent is always to harm you.

Court Strategy: When he gets you angry enough by doing something horrible to you or your children, and you react appropriately, he will discredit you as 'defective', and the psychopath will make himself out to be the victim.

Court Strategy: He will blame you for everything with no proof to back it up. The psychopath will do anything or say anything to win.

Court Strategy: Fight for full custody. If you gain full custody of your children you have a chance to lead a more normal life than if you and your children are forced to endure shared custody. Shared custody with psychopaths means 50% more time to abuse you and your children. If you get full custody, your children will not be as damaged as the children who are forced through the courts to have regular contact with a psychopath parent. More time with a psychopathic parent will mean more time for the children in therapy.

🏛 **Court Strategy**: The psychopaths' favorite defense: Parental Alienation Syndrome. They will accuse you of abusing the children by lying and 'alienating' the children from their father. They will fight for you to lose all custody rights. The courts have put children in the custody of the psychopath even in cases in which police records and testimony by teachers and therapists supported the mother. Do not think he will not use this or win with this strategy. The psychopaths' lies and their ability to convince are exceptional. Prepare against it.

STORY OF D

"He used his friends and work associates to seize the spotlight as the victim. He convinced everyone he knew that I was the abuser. He talked of evidence, but his legal case was built on everything but evidence and fairness. His goal was to win and when he discredited me and destroyed me, he viewed it as a bonus!"

🏛 **Court Strategy**: In a trial, the attorney should prepare for a convincing liar who uses charm and plays the victim. This is a lethal combination to a jury or judge as psychopaths will appear credible and the judge may feel sorry for them. Their premeditated strategy will be to explain away abuse by saying it never happened, you are a liar, you provoked it or you are unstable and he genuinely feels sorry for you. Either way, you will be on trial, not the abuser. When this occurs, your attorney should confront him with continuous questioning and attempt to reveal him as a liar. The goal is to have your attorney get the psychopath to become frustrated and show his anger and abusive nature to the judge.

As Robert Hare states:

> "Psychopaths are social predators who charm, manipulate, and ruthlessly plow their way through life, leaving a broad trail of broken hearts, shattered expectations, and empty wallets. Completely lacking in conscience and in feelings for others, they selfishly take what they want and do as they please, violating social norms and expectations without the slightest sense of guilt or regret."

Do not expect the family court system to make proper decisions for the children in cases with a psychopath because their concern for the best interests of the children is based on honesty and the psychopath will blur the reality due to his inherent nature of dishonesty.

Psychopaths will continue to go unnoticed and unaccountable and families and children will continue to suffer until the courts, therapists, mediators and attorneys recognize the traits of a socially skilled psychopath. Once psychopaths are recognized and held accountable for who they are and what they do, then and only then can the words in the reflecting pool at the Supreme Court Building become a reality for all people suffering at the hands of a psychopath: REASON, HONOR, INTEGRITY, WISDOM, PEACE, PASSION, JUSTICE, COMPASSION, EQUALITY and TRUTH.

CHAPTER EIGHT

PARENTING WITH A PSYCHOPATH

~⟨○⟩~

"IF YOU CAN'T BE A GOOD EXAMPLE, YOU'LL HAVE TO SETTLE
FOR BEING A HORRIBLE WARNING."

*B*y virtue of psychopaths' nature, they will create a
dysfunctional family. Psychopaths are almost always unaware of any true and real connection with their children, or their
effect on them. In cases of families, the time lost to a destructive
psychopath is time lost forever and lives typically will have been
compromised. The legacy of a psychopath can last for a lifetime.

The most important priority for a child should be the right to live
in an environment where the child is cared for, treated fairly, and
loved. Without these things, the child will not 'connect' and will
be emotionally vulnerable and may be fair game to any psychopath
and their abuse.

Most often, however, children are forced by the courts to spend half
their time with a damaged psychopathic parent, based on the fact
that "he is the parent." When the courts take the children from
a safe and functional environment and place them into a psychopath's life, the children will begin to believe that the psychopath
father must be OK or why would the 'law' enforce time spent with
him. This typically creates conflict with the children and may lead

them to view you as being 'disruptive' instead of protective. Even more damaging than being taken out of a loving and safe home, is the fact that now the children are in a situation with a parent they cannot trust and cannot turn to when issues arise due to insecurity, lack of trust and an inability to maintain connectedness.

The courts will not hesitate to split the child between two homes, all the while not realizing that a major consequence of this is the disruption of family traditions that have been created to keep the family connected. To 'start again' with new traditions is not impossible, but it creates a sense of loss and disruption within the family. When a parent acts crazy and creates unsettling and provocative circumstances, this prevents the child from being connected and, in fact, creates disconnection. This disruption in the family is what the psychopath thrives on and encourages.

Important: When children become teenagers, the motivation to do what is right comes from being connected to a group larger than themselves which typically is family, school, friends, sport teams, and other extracurricular groups. The 'group' that the teens identify with is important. Often a psychopathic parent will remove the teen from a group so the child is easier to control. Often the first thing the psychopath will fight to change is to get his child out of sports teams as the coaches can be strong allies to the child and the normal parent. The group will help the teen see the psychopath for what he is and, therefore, the group is the enemy to the psychopath. It is common to see the psychopath convince therapists, teachers, and courts that the groups are a stressor to the child and that it takes up too much time and it is the group, not the psychopath, that is responsible for the change in grades or the sudden depression. He is likely to blame the group to deflect any blame from his own behaviors.

Again, if the psychopath manages to separate the child from a social or sports group, he is in a good position to continue his reign of disruption of the routine. Along with disrupting the routine, he will count on the child's self esteem suffering from being disconnected from the team or group. Disconnected children may fall prey to depression, drug use, and low self-esteem. Individuals with low self-esteem are easier to abuse.

Once they are ordered to spend more time with the psychopath, the child will learn anti-social behaviors, lies, and manipulation. Further, they will not learn what is right and moral by watching the behavior of the psychopath. If the psychopath's group, and now the child's primary group, includes his current wife or girlfriend and their damaged extended family and the friends hanging on for money, they will reinforce unacceptable standards of behavior. If a child connects with this group, he or she will learn to take on its traits.

Unfortunately, he will become a role model for the children the more time they spend with him. Often the children will begin to make excuses for his deviant and anti social behavior and the young children may take on some of his behaviors like smoking, watching porn, drinking beer, swearing, lying, and all forms of racism.

The children will see that the psychopath is defined and motivated more by his possessions and power than by love, compassion and truth, which have no meaning for him at all. Feeling understood requires empathy, which we know psychopaths cannot feel. A psychopath cannot love and does not know how to show love in the context of 'normal' behavior. Most often, his current wife or other enabler tells him he 'should' react this way or say the things that convey compassion or love. Left to his own devices, he will not be able to feel or react in an appropriate way, as he is incapable of feeling it.

There are many ways in which you can teach and show your child love that the psychopath cannot: love from family, connections to school and community, spirituality, consistent responsibility at home, participation in sports, caring for and loving pets, nature and respect for it, as well as beauty and the arts. Learn to tolerate your children's feelings of unhappiness and they will more likely share how they feel. Teach them that, instead of shame and anger, the response to adversity is to reach out. You can teach them to deal with adversity by proving you can find a solution. This will be difficult if the psychopath has convinced the children you are damaged, untrustworthy or a liar. If this is the case, then the children will feel they have nowhere to turn.

STORY OF D

"He feels superior to his children. In a way he made them feel inferior…he needed to. It was conditional love. As much as I tried to help him see his children differently, he could not recognize them as individuals. He neglected their true nature. It was as if he was playing a game—the parenting game. He played a role without any emotion and connection. The words sounded right but the meaning behind it was distorted and somehow wrong. This was his position of power over his kids. He projected an image and tried to become the parent he thought was correct. When I called him on it, he raged on me and then changed for a while as if he was 'acting.' But he always went back to the way it was. He developed a strategy. He spent time and effort to lie to everyone about his relationship to the children. Even the children believed him at times."

A PSYCHOPATH AND THE CHILDREN

- Psychopaths are always poorly qualified to effectively parent.
- Psychopaths' relentless criticism teaches the child they can never be good enough and this becomes a way for the psychopath to demand more and more from your child. This leads to self-esteem issues as the child matures.
- Psychopaths have failed to develop a conscience, are unable to experience guilt or remorse, have a difficult time monitoring their behavior and give no thought to its effects on others and, as such, they become a distorted role model. Their psychopathic behaviors are being learned, as 'what real men are like, the kind of men your mother hates.' This creates unnecessary and costly separation between mother and child.
- Their needs are far more important to them than the child's. They need constant recognition and admiration from the child regardless of what the child needs.
- The psychopathic need for power will always come first.
- They are suspicious and the child will experience a lack of trust from the psychopath regardless of the reality. The child will be 'grilled' constantly and psychopaths will always expect the worst from the child.
- They will bestow rewards if the child does what they want. If the child does not obey the psychopaths' rules and demands, the child will feel immediate retaliation.
- They will attempt and most likely succeed in removing children from the mother. If the psychopath creates enough conflict, most therapists will recommend to the court that the children be removed from both homes. Boarding schools are a popular option.
- They will use fear to get the child to behave in a cer-

tain way: i.e. "If you don't live with me, I will hurt your mother."

- Psychopaths will always silence those opinions that differ from theirs.
- They need to be in total control and any attempts the child makes to separate his or her identity from the psychopath, will result in immediate disapproval and psychological abuse.
- They will lie constantly and any attempts the child makes at correcting the lie will bring harsh punishment. This will teach the child to lie or, at the very least, to accept liars.
- The psychopath's impatience is ever-present and this creates stress for the child.
- Neglecting their development and basic needs is common. The child will learn to not value his own needs.

Psychopaths will eventually lose respect from their children but this may take years, because the damage the children suffer will delay normal psychological maturity.

Story of M

"It took me years to leave him, but as I look back on it now, I don't know why it took so long. I should have left him when I was pregnant. He told me he did not want the baby but acted so excited when other people were around. He refused to touch me throughout the pregnancy and called me a "fat chick" when I was 6 months pregnant. He watched porn every night after the news and laughed when I told him it made me uncomfortable. Once the baby was born, he would stay out all night and take prolonged trips. He would take a 3-day business trip to London and extend it for a week and play in Paris; all without letting me know where he was. He needed the freedom and didn't want a wife who was "needy"…you know one who "needed" to know where he was while in Europe. He never asked about the baby or me while he was away and his indifference was painful."

Story of A

"Their father admitted in therapy and later to the children's therapist that he had changed and was in full agreement with the proposed plans of the children's therapist. The therapist was so enthralled with him that even two years later, after he had not followed through with any of his suggestions for the children the therapist still said 'He has made progress' 'He listens to me.' His long-winded monologues and dominance with the therapist only added to the therapist's conclusions that he was "trying" and should get more time with the children. He used psychotherapy to learn concepts, key words and superficial insight—all designed to be able to manipulate more effectively. He continues to defy the therapist's recommendations for the children. The children's therapist is still supporting him due to the therapist's inability to see that he was indeed gullible to a common psychopath."

Story of M

"I overcompensated with my child to offset his neglect and abuse. I tried to soothe my child's anger and hurt. I micro managed the situation in order to keep it sane. I felt that if I tried harder to help by controlling and changing their father's abusive behavior, we would all be better off. Working and cooperating with others is how I had always created some of my greatest wins or triumphs. But no matter how hard I tried I could not get what I wanted most: a peaceful and united family which included the father. We were all in so much pain. We could not see a way through it and he continued to hurt us immeasurably."

STORY OF L

"As time went on, I struggled with my health, as the negative emotions were permeating my cells. My emotional and physical health was suffering. If it had only been me who was suffering, I would have chosen to move on. But, because my children were also suffering at the hands of their father, I could not move them forward without him. I felt I needed to try to change him for their sake. It was one of my biggest mistakes *and* had far reaching consequences with my children. My goal became to not have any feelings toward the abuser and reconcile so we could co-parent for the children's sake. This was great in concept—to minimize the time I spent angry for the sake of the children. What I did not count on was how often the children would be hurt and that they came to rely on me to help them sort through their grief. I was consistently thrown into the middle of the conflict between the children and their father."

To parent with a psychopath will be your most difficult endeavor. There may be years when your children will believe the psychopath's lies and manipulations and turn against you. Your children will go through very dark times at the hands of a psychopath and you will be forced to stand by, as you may not have any recourse to protect. The psychopath will eventually age and as they do, they remain sick but the children, now adults themselves, will take pity on them and may no longer view them as an abuser. They may choose to forget their past at the hands of a psychopath and concentrate on the present. Do not wait or expect any huge revelations from the children. It may be too painful for them to recall their past and they may need to create a new past that has no basis in reality. Remember that this process is theirs, not yours.

As a good parent, in spite of the psychopathic influence on your children, you know the values to live by. Remember to show your children trust. Give trust and receive their trust. Be self-aware and praise your children for correct thinking and correct choices. Help them to stay connected to a source higher than themselves. Be inspirational and focus your life on a higher purpose. Do not let yourself become a victim of a psychopath. Do not teach defeat. Save yourself. What is most important for those who have children, is that once you 'save' yourself, you are then able to save them. And, believe me, if their father is a psychopath, they will need you to show them a way to be and how to protect themselves and create a new reality for themselves as well. You cannot help them do this until you do it for yourself first! Show your children, through your own example, how to embrace life and live life in spite of difficulties and obstacles...or precisely because of them.

CHAPTER NINE

MOVING ON AND
NEW BEGINNINGS

"Every growth moment has a beginning...a starting point so to speak."

*N*o one who has survived a psychopath would underestimate the challenge that lies in front of someone who falls prey to a life with one. When we get to a place in which we feel ready to move on, we have survived the psychopath. Now is the time, the beginning, of saving ourselves. We now have an opportunity to start again. Finding strength and balance is what will save us.

Understand that we could not have done otherwise at any given point in time. Each moment builds upon the previous moment. Our thoughts, words, feelings and actions are powerful beyond our knowing. The destructive behavior patterns that created the drama we experienced, no longer has to be "our way of being." The patterns of fear, greed and corruption, which created our pain and suffering, cannot be sustained when we are focused on truth, forgiveness and love. It is critical that we all stay focused on the truth.

It may seem that we have been propelled into one drama after another. In the midst of such dramatic changes, it is difficult, when managing a psychopath's destruction on our lives, to stay focused on the positive things we want to create in our lives and the lives of our children. We can however, make it our priority to become strong, independent and peaceful.

We can prevent ourselves from becoming overwhelmed with the extreme situations surfacing all around us, and we can change what is happening in our lives. We can become the calm in the eye of the storm. No matter how stressful your life is at this moment, know that you have all of the skill, knowledge, courage, wisdom, and strength you need to move forward. Regardless of how helpless or hopeless you feel facing a psychopath, out of the adversity you can transform into your highest vision of yourself.

This may seem easy enough, but a psychopath will sense our newfound strength and he will fight it, because in order to win, the psychopath needs us to be weak, controllable and scared. And, if the psychopath is no longer in our life, our memories of the suffering, left unchecked could destroy our future. We must make every effort to move on.

Our only hope is to heal ourselves and make ourselves happy and peaceful.

STORY OF L

"Today my health is good. My children love me. I have good friends. I have my dogs and cats that are happy. I am smart and will find a way to create a better reality for myself."

"I used to tell my children that every day held infinite possibilities. At the time I said this, I had enough money to stay home and raise my children, and was enjoying the superficial happiness that comes from thinking money buys happiness and protects you. But the infinite possibilities comment was valuable. I think of it now. Infinite possibilities. It means that I can choose anything at any time. I remind myself to choose something today that will make me feel better than the hopeless thoughts I awoke to. Infinite possibilities. It means that not only can I create some meaning, peace and joy in my life at any moment of my choosing, it also means that life or God or 'some force greater than myself' can also be creating something good for me. I feel hope."

"I try to let this tiny feeling of hopefulness get a little bigger. I stop the urge to destroy this feeling with more 'but what about the …' thoughts. I go with the hope feeling. I hope things are better today. I hope a solution presents itself for some of the worries and problems I have. I hope that I keep myself healthy today by taking a walk. I hope I keep my thoughts positive today by exerting some willpower to stop the fearful thoughts."

"I remember when my life was different and there were no worries about survival. I remember having worries and fears that were different. There were worries of losing my money. There was the fear of being taken advantage of because I had money. There was the worry of finding real love and the worry that my children would never learn the value of hard work and service to others. There was a time when I was faced with adversity, but with more resources. Once the money was used for attorneys, my reality has shifted to helping just myself. But I know well enough that helping myself means I will be able to help others eventually."

ENDING SUFFERING

"SUFFERING DISSOLVES WHEN I STOP LOOKING AT IT. SUFFERING STOPS WHEN I STOP FIGHTING WITH IT."

You survived the destruction at the hands of a psychopath and it is unnecessary to continue to destroy your sense of peace and personal power by continuing to allow yourself to relive the horror. Releasing the memories, the hurt and suffering of being with a psychopath is essential before you can move on. Hanging on to the pain and giving it importance in your life will prolong your suffering. We know how to do it. When you feel pain while exercising, you pause, reevaluate and either stop or change what you are doing. The pain is an indicator of the need for a change in direction. The solution to the situation you are faced with is no different. It is imperative that when you feel pain, you stop thinking of the memory immediately. Change the direction of your thoughts. Dealing with the memories of a psychopath's devastation in your life will create pain. It is critical for you to place the painful memories and thoughts on pause and evaluate if this is something you need to continue to think about. If it is just creating pain and nothing can be changed, then STOP thinking about it immediately. Change what you are doing. Know that a new direction is needed. Painful and negative thoughts can dissolve with a simple shift of thought and direction. We can eliminate suffering for ourselves by stopping negative thoughts.

Your memories will continue to keep you rooted in the past when your memories contain fear, anxiety, sadness, and anger. Your present will continue to be filled with discomfort. These are your choices now: to release the painful memories or continue to let them define your present reality. When you allow yourself to recall a fearful memory, you pull yourself out of balance. Your body feels like it did when it first occurred. When you feel the pain, let it be a signal to change the way you felt in the past. Thoughts precede action and, to move forward and regain your life, it is imperative to disrupt your negative thoughts or memories from the past. To let the fear go and replace it with a positive thought will be extremely difficult to do. Your happiness, peace and balance however, depend upon your ability to be strong enough to change your thoughts.

All of us suffer. I used to believe it inevitable and the best we could hope for was how to learn to suffer less. I believe now that we can eliminate suffering for ourselves to a large degree by releasing the emotions and thoughts we carry with us that are negative and ultimately destructive. It is a heavy burden to carry around these past thoughts, memories and missed opportunities. Over the years, they become heavy. To lighten the 'load' seems simple enough, yet difficult at best.

If we keep in mind that painful and difficult experiences lead to growth, then it makes sense that suffering shows us an area where we have not yet grown, where we need to grow. This is the process for transformation and change.

Story of L

"I feel as if my old patterns of fear are no longer able to pull me off center the way they once did, and my psychopath cannot manipulate me through fear the way he used to. I am relieved that it is the psychopath, not me, who is fragmented and dysfunctional."

ENDING FEAR

"FEAR CEASES TO BE THE MAIN EVENT IN MY LIFE WHEN I STOP LOOKING FOR IT."

Fear seems to run most encounters in our world. There is the fear of death, fear of rejection, fear of losing someone or fear of losing all our 'stuff.' Fear is used to control people in the media, churches and schools. Because fear is contagious, it can control the masses almost effortlessly. Doubt, jealousy, sadness, and anger all lead to the path of fear. The psychopath uses these negative emotions and needs you to be feeling one or all of them at all times. Negativity means becoming more dominated and it is easy to submit to it out of fear and insecurity. To be negative is easy. When you face negativity, it generally will produce fear. This fear can pull you out of balance and create some major disruptions in your life. We all walk in the midst of darkness at some time; how can we not fall prey to its influence? Be disciplined and let the fear go and create a thought of love in its place. To uphold your integrity and stay balanced is not an easy task.

Story of A

"Fear is an unrecognized outcome. Nothing has happened. He is threatening to do something to the children and me but today nothing has actually happened. There is nothing to have the emotion of fear about. I remind myself to do my work and keep my emotions positive and directed at what I find acceptable and this will pass quickly. "

When fear is allowed to dominate your thoughts or body, they may produce depression, disease and discomfort. Negative thoughts, at the very best, distract you from your purpose and can hinder you from moving forward on your path.

Story of D

"In some cases in my life it was impossible for me to function normally for years, until the feelings of victimization and pain were reduced to a workable level. Then I could finally breathe through the thoughts without constriction and indigestion. Yes, indigestion. I would feel the fear and the thought or memory of it would fill me like hot air...I felt physically full; unable to swallow or breathe deeply. I experienced shallow breathing and labored speech. I will never underestimate how difficult it is to manage the fear of a psychopath."

Many of you who choose to hold onto the old beliefs based in negativity will feel emotional, distraught, angry, frustrated and lost. Hopefully when you feel the pain, you will see it as a challenge to let go of the old, limited way of being. Every thought and action you have will be manifested into your physical body. In other words, what you think is what you become. You have the ability to choose to be happy or emotionally sad. The reason this simple concept and comment is so powerful is that you can virtually change your biology with these principles. For example, when you release tension through laughter, it creates physical, emotional, and mental balance.

Before you call it bad or good, think of the fact that 'this too shall pass.' This will comfort you in times of suffering and it will make you aware of the fleeting aspect of every situation. This lessens the pain and allows you to suffer less and enjoy more. Be aware of the reality that "at this moment I am creating suffering for myself." This will open infinite possibilities through awareness. It will create more intelligent ways of dealing with the situation.

ENDING BLAME

As you begin to let go of painful memories, you can begin to stop blaming the psychopath. This will be difficult, as there is so much for which to blame a psychopath. But remember, you are healing and before you can heal, it is imperative that you stop your internal blame cycle in order to survive. Taking responsibility for your thoughts and actions will help you to overcome the many challenges in your life.

Before being able to move out of this horrendous situation you find yourself in, identify who it is that put you into this situation. Yes, that person is you. If you continue to be stuck in the blame cycle, you will not be able to move past this. Because of the nature of the abuse you have suffered from a psychopath, it is easy to blame and few would argue that you 'deserve' to point fingers. However, when looking at the cycle or the big picture, it is important to recognize the part you played and will continue to play.

When you think about it, no one is ever going to take care of yourself, but yourself. Your attorney, pastor, friends or family will lend support, but they will not ultimately be responsible or effective in rescuing you from yourself. Ending blame is imperative for healing to begin. Every single moment, we are either empowering ourselves with positive thoughts or contributing to our suffering by blame, depending on the focus of our attention.

STORY OF L

"I wish I had understood a long time ago that I had no control over his abuse and unhealthy decisions. I would have had a different outcome—not necessarily for my children, but for me. I realized that my anger and hurt had to become a constant in my life. Even hurts that were years old still hurt as if *they* happened yesterday."

When you feel victimized, remember that whatever happens to you is not who you are, it is what is happening to you. This subtle distinction of who you are versus what is happening to you can be dramatic in terms of your recovery. How you choose to respond will create who you are. These circumstances are revealing. Will you respond or react? We are responsible for creating our experiences. We can accomplish a profound transformation by choosing positive thoughts, words, actions and feelings.

STORY OF M

"Eventually I resigned myself to believing that the abuse wouldn't end. Life was forcing me to change in a direction that I didn't want to go. I stopped trusting everything would work out. The danger of another attack from him was always lurking and I became afraid of the future. I didn't feel safe. I didn't know how to move forward. When I look back now, I can see there was nothing to feel guilty about and no one to blame. There is also no one to hate, but I can see clearly that there is much that could have been avoided had I understood this earlier."

Let's go through some typical You's that are used to blame the psychopath:

1. YOU lied to me
2. YOU abused me
3. YOU ruined my life

Yes, this is all true. However, this next step is necessary to move past the control of a psychopath. The negative energy you send out always comes back to you. Have you ever realized that a negative thought can actually hurt you the minute you have it? These thoughts keep this ugly and hurtful energy inside of you. So, you may have removed the psychopath from your home, but his energy is still in your body and mind. Your job is to get rid of it all!

Anger and blame can lead to either constructive or destructive outcomes. Negative emotions of all types that are expressed over injustices, can cause individuals to change or can cause more pain. Anger can be used to motivate you to greater possibilities or be manifested as resentment and revenge. Anger as a lifestyle includes people who are litigious, mean-spirited, and irritable, and these people can erode a peaceful and happy life. The effect of negative emotions can be debilitating and some never recover from an encounter with an angry psychopath.

But in order to move past this pain, anger, and suffering, YOU must be able to say:

1. I allowed myself to be lied to.
2. I stayed in an abusive relationship
3. I gave him the opportunity to ruin my life

Ouch. I know this hurts. So many 'but, I didn't know,' 'but I couldn't leave,' 'but I had to fight to protect my children,' will come gushing forward. This is ok. Give your mind time to get it all out. Write it down. Write down all the hurts and blames. I know the list will be long. Letting go of the blame and taking responsibility is necessary and difficult. As you begin to let go of old beliefs, you can take responsibility for your own actions and stop blaming others for the events in your life or the lessons you are learning. Again, finding peace and balance will be your hardest task. This will take some time.

Story of L

"I lost sight *of the fact* that I could control my feelings regarding the situation. Instead, I tried to control the actions of the ex. I realized that needing to change him was the biggest ingredient in my continued suffering. After spending energy, time and precious care and concern, I felt resentful and angry that it did not change anything. In fact, it made the situation worse. I had to stop wasting my time trying to change someone who did not want to change."

It may take a long time to accomplish what I have just asked of you. We may struggle and then make huge progress and other times feel as if we are going backwards. Know your own beliefs and common sense values. Of course, once you start on this path, you will go forward—it just won't feel like it at times. Persevere.

Taking responsibility for your thoughts and actions will propel you into a new way of thinking and living. Imagine overcoming any and all challenges in your life and doing so effortlessly. Think then, of being grateful for the struggle that motivated you into an entire new experience! When you are able to release old beliefs that have caused you pain through judgment and perhaps violence toward yourself or others, you are then able to entertain thoughts that are pure inspiration because they are based in love. When you can do this you are on your way to accepting that you are truly blessed and are never alone. Instead of blaming evil, bring light into the situation. I expect great things when I begin to become responsible for my choices.

ENDING JUDGMENT

When you experience judgment in your thoughts toward yourself or others, set those thoughts aside. If you can admit, without judgment or blame, that you did not get what you wanted: a decent parent for your children, a happy marriage, a safe home, you can begin to heal. Try to view the situation from a non-judgmental perspective. This is always harder than it sounds.

Story of **M**

"It continues to surprise me when I come face to face with the judgment of others. Sometimes it was just an off-handed comment and sometimes it was a hurtful case of being left out of social gatherings. Friends knew the struggle I was in and it was too ugly for them to continue to be involved with. Nothing was ever said outright, but within a year, my social life had changed completely. I have learned the hard way that judgment can really hurt and I have vowed to end my own tendencies to judge others."

You may find that it is easier to label someone than it is to find an inner resolution to the conflict. I am not advocating resolution directly with someone, as there are psychopaths with whom you cannot reason. I am talking about inner resolution. Changing your thoughts regarding the person or situation. When you are busy judging, blaming, hating, you are incapable of moving past the stuck situation before you.

All judgment, even the judgment that is justifiable, is part of the hate that will only hurt you. We do need protection from the courts and better ways to protect ourselves, but along with these, we need to end the judgment in response to the conflict that psychopaths create in our lives. I know. I never said this was going to be easy.

CHANGING OUR THOUGHTS

It is difficult to let go of the negative thoughts. They have been your companions for so long, they have become a habit. If thoughts do create your reality, be aware of the thoughts and feelings in your body that keep the pain, grief and sadness in place. Think about what you are sharing with others currently. We have all shared depression, anger, and sadness and if you believe that you can only give to others that which you have inside of yourself, it makes sense that when you share grief or fear, it is what you are thinking and feeling at the time.

STORY OF A

"There was never a time that I did not battle the negative and self-defeating thoughts. There always seemed to be something troubling enough to wake me up. I was never so full of myself as when I was in pain."

For some, pain can help propel you in a new direction. But how many times must we endure pain or hit the proverbial bottom before we allow ourselves to move past the suffering?

Some of the most debilitating feelings arise from thinking of the 'what ifs' from our past. The remembrance of the 'I remember', or 'I used to' thoughts can sabotage your present state. Instead of focusing on what is not working in your life, try concentrating on changing your thoughts. It takes discipline to keep your thoughts focused on the present moment. I say to myself out loud, "Stop!" if I need to get my own attention. Refuse to think about the current issue you are facing and stop running that 'movie' you have in your head of the painful past with the psychopath.

STORY OF L

"I wanted to only share love and peace regardless of what drama I was experiencing at the time, but I allowed my negative emotions to be my gift instead of love and peace."

When I tell you that your thoughts create your reality, understand that hateful thoughts create hateful emotions to be passed on to others through your actions. Viewing it in this way may help you to work harder at controlling your thoughts. You cannot hide your true thoughts from the world for long.

STORY OF M

"I want to share love with the world, not my baggage from the ex. We all know people who at first meeting are all smiles and sweetness. Then if you have a follow up conversation or delve into a deeper level of communication, it is easy to see that behind the superficial sweetness *are* lies, anger and jealousy. I am moving past those dramas now."

For the love of God, do not hang onto your bitterness, anger, and pain for a moment longer. Instead of devising new ways to deceive those you meet as to your hurtful past, create a new reality for yourself with new, positive thoughts. No matter how real your challenges seem or how victimized you may feel due to your experiences with financial limitations, illness, low self-esteem, loveless relationships, hatred, unfairness, ignorance, etc., those parts of our 'past' life can continue only if we continue to give life to them through our thoughts. No matter what life gives you, you can choose to respond in a new way.

STORY OF D

"I try to remember *that* my thoughts create my reality and yet, right now, I am choosing to live in fear. I argue with myself that thoughts are not as powerful and reliable as action and the more I defended that point the more I was stuck in the same patterns. Thoughts do change something. I know they do. I try again to begin to think differently. I remind myself that I am safe."

The mental picture you have of yourself cannot be overstated. The belief you hold about yourself will create the thoughts you have and ultimately the action you will create. Start with creating a new belief of who you are. Ask yourself exactly who you are. Remember who you are….this will help set you free from the fears and dramas. Make the situation you are going through look perfect in your head: the perfect outcome, the perfect conversation, and the perfect response. Give this your full attention. This line of thinking should ease some of the anxiety and turmoil you are currently feeling. Keep this positive picture of who you are (or how you want to be) in your mind. Refer to it often. It is the new you. From this new vantage point, all things are possible.

STORY OF A

"It is not a result of the actions that were happening to me as I thought, but what I chose to keep inside of me that determined how I felt. I tried to make the choice to be no one's victim any longer. I knew I had to choose my own happiness over his power plays and manipulations. Once he died, he had no power over me any longer. I felt free. If he hadn't died, I don't know if I could have survived."

Once you are able to change your negative thoughts to positive thoughts and take responsibility for what happened, the control you will have over your emotions and ultimately what you create in your life, will lead to a new reality for yourself that includes the fact that:

1. You can't be upset unless you allow it.
2. You can't be manipulated unless you allow it
3. You can't be controlled unless you allow it
4. You can't be angry unless you allow it.

What a relief to know you are finally in control! The psychopath no longer has control of you, unless you allow it. You can choose to be peaceful, joyous, and safe.

As long as you direct your thoughts toward love, peace, beauty, and kindness, you will be able to take control back and then choose what you will think and how you will choose to react. The choice is always yours. You have thousands of opportunities to change and influence your life every day. Yes, thousands of thoughts enter your mind and you can choose to let them stay and create stress and sadness or, with love, move them out with a simple nudge into the light.

Remember, it's only thoughts…your thoughts. You are responsible for what you create. If you choose to express negative thoughts and keep your pattern of control, then this will be returned to you. You have the ability. The choice is yours. Make the choice. Choose to be free of your negative and troubling thoughts. Send them away and be free.

FORGIVENESS
"EVIL IS UNCONSCIOUSNESS. WITH FORGIVENESS, TRUE POWER EMERGES."

Forgiving an abuser is hard.

Again and again, we are told to forgive. What does this mean? How can we? What does it mean if you don't want to forgive him? What if you feel he doesn't deserve to be forgiven after what did to you or your children?

The process toward forgiveness is the same for everyone. You may ask "How can having forgiveness be the same for someone who has lost a child by the hands of another, versus someone who has been lied to by a friend?" It would seem logical to have 'forgiveness heavy' and 'forgiveness lite' for instances such as these. But, in my experience, I have found that the process of forgiveness is the same in every situation. It's the willingness to forgive that is difficult. It involves a person's willingness--the desire to forgive--that is hard or easy, not the process of forgiveness.

Forgiveness is possible when you recognize that the thoughts and emotions of your painful past that you have been hanging onto are only hurting you--not the abuser. When you are ready to make a new decision about those thoughts, forgiveness is possible.

And once we can understand and forgive, our personal well being can thrive.

STORY OF M

"I was stuck in the cycle of abuse and pain as it was recurring for years. It was hard to find the time and space to deal with one set of circumstances and begin the process of forgiveness when the next onslaught of drama and betrayal was on its heels. At times over the years since the divorce, I was able to forgive and release hurts through work with a spiritual teacher or gifted therapist. But, the hurts continued. It made moving forward difficult as the attacks kept coming. I felt as if I had failed to protect my child from her father's abuse. I lacked the skills to forgive."

Every one of us can remember a time when they were treated unfairly, hurt in some way, or lied to. A life with a psychopath typically includes years of abuse, manipulation, and lies. However, if you are alive, you are dealing with issues that beg for forgiveness.

STORY OF L

"I have tried to 'forgive' my ex for 20 years of suffering. When I tried to forgive, he viewed my forgiveness and the attempts at compromise as a weakness. He then used my vulnerable state as an opportunity to hurt me again and again. When I forgave, I seemed to give my power away and was hurt again. In my attempts to forgive, I felt as if I was condoning his unkindness or, worse yet, minimizing my own pain and trauma. Was there a middle ground? The picture I had of being a great parent and raising wonderful children took a hit. It became impossible to have what I envisioned because of the behavior of their father. My dream was being destroyed as surely as my children were. How could I recover from the loss of my children's innocence, the loss of my dream of a happy and healthy family? I was not prepared for a loss of this magnitude; a loss that would go on for 20 years. I not only lost the family experience I wished for, I lost friendships that could not and would not endure the story as it unfolded year after year. I lost precious years of happiness to the loss and anger that would follow. I was so stuck in pain and trying to shield my children from the onslaught of sickness from their father that I lost faith. I lost track of where I wanted to go in my life. I lost the ability to see past the pain and daily drama. And life still went on. Where was the magic combination of forgetting the painful acts and forgiving the abuser?"

What is Forgiveness?

1. It is for you only--not the abuser
2. It is giving yourself the power--not the abuser
3. It is about healing yourself--no longer a victim and no longer letting your health suffer with unresolved issues.

You can't go from hurt to forgiveness without work. We must recognize and honor our hurt feelings. But there is balance to be found here as well. We must be certain to allow grieving to take place, but we must have balance and know that this will pass.

STORY OF D

"I tried to lessen the impact he had on us but, without forgiveness, I had a hard time overcoming my feelings of victimization. I spent years trying to change him with the expectation that he would then stop abusing the children and me. I was filled with justifiable anger and hurt. I had to realize I had no control over his abusive behavior toward the children. Forgiveness was the means to minimize the effects of his suffering in our lives. Was I to pray to God that I be forgiven for not being able to forgive my ex? I judged myself harshly as I hadn't learned how to forgive. My mother's family was non-college educated, Italian immigrants and they held grudges and never talked deeply about their feelings. They were not good role models for forgiveness. My church talked about it, but never gave concrete examples on how to do it. I never knew forgiveness could be taught like any skill you desire to have."

Forgiveness can allow you to feel less anger. It doesn't stop you from being angry at his actions, but it can stop you from damaging yourself...from altering your reaction because of a psychopath's actions. We must recognize that we do not have control over other's actions and we must forgive ourselves for trying to control even if you believe it is for someone's best interests.

STORY OF L

"I always wished that their father would be a good parent. Unfortunately, insisting on him being a good parent had disastrous consequences. As I insisted on wanting something that would never happen, I became more and more upset. I knew my children would be hurt if he did not change and I tried to change him. My wish for him to be a better parent turned into an expectation that I felt obligated to enforce. The pain this action caused me and the boys *was* immeasurable. I tried to get him to stop allowing the children to consume alcohol at 9 years old. I tried to stop him from verbally abusing them. I tried to stop him from physical hurting them. I tried to stop him from abandoning them for long periods at a time. I tried to stop him from having sex with their caregivers. I tried to stop him from being a narcissist. I used therapists, schoolteachers, the courts, any means I could to help my children. I tried harder and harder. But through all of it, I realized I did not have the power to make it go away or get better. I suffered. My children suffered. "

"In order to forgive and move past this hurt I had to change the way I thought of this and not focus on changing their father. I knew it was proper to wish or hope for him to be a better father. It was not proper thinking I *could* demand that he be a better father. I simply did not have the power to make him a better parent. I thought the courts would, but they, too, did not have the power to change him. No therapist had the power to change his behavior. Only he could change himself and he refused. This left us a list of grievances and hurts that were devastating. I had to find a way to forgive and let these feelings go. I had to put this loss in a perspective that would allow me to move on. I realized that I could not have a close relationship with the children while I was intent on protecting them from their father's abuse and by fighting their father. The struggle was hurting us all and most importantly, hurting my relationship with my children. I had to move the remembrances of the past abuses to the side so I had room to forge a new relationship with my children. Every time I reacted with anger and hurt to something their father did, I was hurting my children. I had to use the love I had for my children as motivation to change the way I was looking at and dealing with their father. I had to forgive their father."

We must find a way to experience forgiveness. Forgiveness is for your well being only. We must find a way to focus on other, more important life goals and desires rather than focusing on revenge, pain, or hurt. We must find a way to recover. If you want to suffer less, you must find peace within yourself. Forgiveness is one way toward personal peace. It is meaningful and necessary.

STORY OF D

"My desire to have peace began to outweigh the desire for revenge or *to* change the offender. I began to want less time devoted to the hurt and the 'fixing of the drama.' I was not comfortable with the feeling that I was becoming a victim to his temper, manipulation, and hatred. I wanted to survive it and move on. I began to feel like I was missing out on fun, peace, and happiness on a day to day basis as I was too consumed with fending off the attacks and trying to make sense of it all to myself and my children. These feelings were the beginning *of my* search for a different resolution. This search gave me the solution of forgiveness."

Over time, with new thought patterns, you can begin to feel less anger and hurt. It does not happen overnight and it still takes conscious work using forgiveness strategies to manage the thoughts as they emerge. You can learn to forgive and move past the feelings that are hurting you.

FORGIVENESS STRATEGIES

1. Quiet your mind with slow breathing and vow to reduce the amount of time you replay the hurts and grievances.

Remember that things could always have been worse. And they were not. Although there was pain and hurt, there were times when there was love and joy. It's Ok to be tattered and bruised, as time will heal this. Remember that you did survive.

2. Practice forgiveness. Forgiveness is a choice that you can make to begin living with peace and appreciation. Forgive for little things and progress from there. When the image of the hurt or betrayal encroaches on your forgiveness moment, begin to breath slowly again and slowly direct your thoughts back to a place of forgiveness. Choose to continue to breathe slowly and replace negative images with loving, forgiving thoughts and images. Journal as a means of expressing and releasing the hurt. List actions that would improve the quality of your life.

3. Focus on the love you feel, have, and can give or receive. Love to one's self and all that lives is the most powerful transformational force of all. Let the love in from everywhere until you feel peaceful. Hold a thought in your mind of a loving moment until you can feel your body begin to relax. When grievances enter into your mind and your body begins to tighten up, turn your attention to the loving thought and place your attention on this. With love, you are able to feel joy and can have a positive attitude in the face of prolonged adversity.

4. Stay focused on your goals. Eventually the difficult and painful circumstances will fall away and you want to have current accomplishments to replace the bitter experiences that made up your past. It is time to let the hurt of the past become an insignificant event in the big picture that is your life. Put your goals, dreams and desires first. Keep the drama at bay. When you focus on your plans, past resentments eventually will become less important.

5. Replace negativity with positive thoughts and intentions.
   Begin slowly with phrases such as, "God bless you" (leaving
   it up to God is always a safe bet). Send negative thoughts
   into the light: "I want to feel good and this is stopping me
   from feeling good, so you must leave now." (a good choice;
   after all, the darkness is where you were), I forgive myself
   for these thoughts and I forgive you.

STORY OF D

"When I dwelled on my horrible circumstances, the situation
seemed to push my goals and plans further and further away from
realization. There were weeks when I didn't even think about goals
and plans I had for myself that were important and gave my life
meaning. I was immersed in pain and lost sight of what peace and
joy meant."

All people experience loss in their lives. All of us feel hurt and angry. We must learn to deal with these emotions and hardships, if for
no other reason than our children watch and what we choose to do,
or not to do, teaches them so much. We can teach our children to
forgive by forgiving their father for his mistakes. We can choose not
to forgive each other and we can watch the devastation in our children. Unforgiveness creates pain and may contribute to the cycle of
abuse in our children's lives.

STORY OF L

"I've heard it said that those people who are bound together in a
lifetime have had many lifetimes together. I can't say for sure if it's
true, all I know is that we are bound together and the love we have
in our hearts will last lifetime after lifetime.

I hope that when my children recall snap shots of their lives that they feel fortunate that they were loved. I hope that they will see what I tried to teach them....being a survivor...a person who was challenged yet triumphant and who was a loving and forgiving role-model for others. I hope that struggle and pain is not all they remember. I hope they see connection, love and gratitude. I hope that through my forgiveness, I was a teacher of strength, conviction and peace."

As adults, we can choose to learn how to forgive others and ourselves. We must understand that we all make bad decisions and make mistakes that we regret. We can learn to take things others do less personally and move quickly through the pain and hurt into forgiveness. The better able we are to help ourselves, the more we are able to show others how to avoid those whose intent is to harm us. It is imperative that we choose to create a forgiving approach to life.

GRATITUDE

YOU ARE ALIVE. YOU ARE ALIVE. TODAY YOU ARE ALIVE. GIVE THANKS FOR THIS.

Think of being grateful for the struggle that motivated you into a new and happier experience! When you are able to release old beliefs that have caused you pain through judgment and blame, you are then on your way towards gratitude.

The strength that comes from being in gratitude cannot be destroyed (unless you allow it) and it can become part of your internal guidance system for making positive choices for yourself. Gratitude comes from its heart-felt goodness. Find it inside yourself and use it always.

I'm here to tell you that you can be thankful for something, no matter how bad it gets. We all know this intellectually, but when in crisis and immersed in pain, it is easy to forget. No matter what is happening to you, I know you can give thanks. Once you give thanks for being alive and the miracle in this, you can begin to move forward. Resist the temptation to focus on what is missing. The 'big 'pile on' I call it. Focusing on what is missing or wrong can dig you deeper into a hell to which you don't need to go.

Give thanks as much as you can. Feel gratitude for everything including, a pet, the sun shining, food in the kitchen, and the simple fact that you are alive. Have gratitude that you overcame major obstacles and you have the ability to do it again, if needed. Give thanks that you survived.

It sounds simplistic, but I will give you a list of things to be thankful for in your darkest hour. Start with these, as I know how hard it is to find gratitude in dark times. Say, "Thank you because…I can breathe, I am not alone, I am clothed, I have food to eat and I am reading this and getting help." Give thanks. I mean deep appreciation right now. Continue this until you can take a full, deep breath.

STORY OF A

"When you have suffered a loss, being thankful is a hard place to come to. "Being thankful for what exactly?" I would say over and over again in my head. I am at the hospital, all alone, with my grief and fear; thankful for what exactly?"

STORY OF D

"I give thanks for learning to count on myself. I give thanks for knowing that what I have to give is enough. I give thanks for learning balance. I give thanks for understanding that it is not my job to fix everyone."

Story of L

"I gave thanks that my children lived through the years of abuse and neglect. I gave thanks for being able to get up to brush my teeth every day when I was suffering from depression. I gave thanks that I was brave enough to write this all down. I am thankful for protecting my children from the worst-case scenarios. I gave thanks for my children, whenever they said 'I love you Mommy.'"

Story of A

"I am grateful for true friends and loyal family. I am grateful for still being alive. I am grateful for the strength to have left him and for surviving. I gave thanks for a friend bringing me dinner when I couldn't afford to go to the grocery store."

Story of M

"I am grateful for my hard earned sense of self. I am grateful I learned how to forgive so that I could survive. I am grateful that I was strong enough to leave him. I gave thanks that I was able to raise my child on my own. I gave thanks that I stopped the drama in my life."

Continue with your list and every day say thank you for something. You know how they say "It's always something..." Well, I like to say, "There's always something to be thankful for." You get the idea.

Feeling gratitude is something you need to be feeling whenever you are doing anything at all. When you are feeling gratitude, you allow joy to flow through you.

COURAGE

"WITH COURAGE, WE HAVE THE ABILITY TO FACE FEAR."

You may feel ordinary, but what you have achieved is extraordinary. How we begin to feel and do extraordinary things takes courage. Surviving a psychopath takes courage. Defending children is courageous. With courage you will find determination and, with enough determination, you will find accomplishment. As survivors of a psychopath, we are courage in motion by the mere fact of our survival and continued existence.

Being able to survive fear and then understand fear, we can now move forward without the anxiety that used to cripple us. When you overcome financial problems and begin to learn something new, start something that benefits others or become creative, this may not be a means to a specific end, but it can be fulfilling in itself.

When you believe that you are the creator of your life, then you are no longer powerless, nor do you see yourself as a victim. At the level of acceptance, you believe you create your own happiness and can see things without misinterpretation.

True courage comes from overcoming the daily, debilitating fear and courage is empowerment.

STORY OF L

"I began to focus on accepting that my life didn't happen according to my plan. I had to change. But now I realized I needed to choose to modify my plans. And this was OK. I didn't want to stay stuck in pain any longer. I chose that my life was going to go on regardless of the outcome of a bad father for my children. It was more important for me to have a good relationship with my children than to keep the resentments from past hurts alive. I chose to give more attention to my relationship with my children and I chose to give less time and energy to the past betrayals and hurts. I knew I could trust myself that if more drama came at me, I would be able to go on. I began to pick myself back up. I began to connect with my old long forgotten and discarded dreams. I began to make peace with the years of drama. It was over. This part was over. I knew I would be able to keep myself safe and happy going forward. I knew that only I could be responsible for how I felt and what I chose to believe and think about. I started to feel less resentment. I stopped living the nightmare. I moved on from the past. I had a new life to create and celebrate."

Do I want the present to be my friend or enemy? It determines the relationship I have with my life. If you allow the present moment to be your friend, you can release the fear, anxiety, expectation, regret, guilt and anger. A daily intention that will help you is: "I want to feel good." This is an important statement and one you may want to use daily for clarity and to bring you into the present. I want to feel good. When you state it simply, you can also hear the answer. Act on your own answer. Listen to yourself, honor your feelings and have the courage to follow your own wise counsel or intuition. See where this takes you.

Know that when you feel your way through any experience and make observations instead of judgments, you can develop a new way of being. This will seem difficult at first attempt, as the psychopath will have destroyed your inner voice. But, we know enough now to remember that any obstacle is only a reminder of the struggle and a sign for a peaceful and safe future. Create yourself anew and with courage, the rest will follow. Listen to your heart and from your newfound and hard-earned beliefs, design your new life.

See the fullness of life all around you. Ask, "What can I give?" Be in service to others.

There is hope that those of us who are survivors of psychopaths will continue to live with understanding and courage and help others suffering in the wake of destruction.

You are courage in motion. Well done.

INFINITE POSSIBILITIES.

Make a prayer, affirmation or mantra to help keep yourself in the present.

I AM AT PEACE TODAY.

I AM HEALING MYSELF.

I AM LIVING MY LIFE IN AWARENESS OF WHAT THE TRUTH IS IN EVERY SITUATION.

I TRUST THAT I AM EXACTLY WHERE I AM MEANT TO BE.

I AM SAFE.

I AM LOVED AND LOVING.

I AM MORE THAN I APPEAR TO BE.

I AM CHANGING AND I AM COMFORTABLE WITH MY LIFE AS IT CHANGES.

I AM HEALTHY IN BODY, MIND AND SPIRIT.

I AM LIVING IN HARMONY WITH ALL LIFE AND NATURE.

I AM A LIVING EXAMPLE OF PERFECT SELF-EXPRESSION.

I AM AT THE RIGHT PLACE AT THE RIGHT TIME FOR MY HIGHEST GOOD.

I AM JOY, HAPPINESS, FORGIVENESS AND GRATITUDE.

ALL IS WELL. ALL IS WELL. ALL IS WELL.